WHAT'S
RIGHT

WHAT'S RIGHT

THE NEW CONSERVATIVE
MAJORITY AND THE
REMAKING OF AMERICA

DAVID FRUM

BasicBooks
A Division of HarperCollins*Publishers*

Grateful acknowledgment is made for permission to reprint, in slightly altered form, from the following:

"Working for the Man," "A Supply-Side Strategy," "Up from Subsidy," "Building Blocks," and "Errors of Commission" from the *American Spectator*. © American Spectator 1995.

"Compassion for Taxpayers," "Living Without the Many Pages of My Life," "Not on My Block," "Not This Quagmire," "The Palaces of Newport," "A Passover Seder," "Peter Taylor," and "The Safety Cult" from the *Financial Post*.

"You're on Your Own" in Part II is reprinted with permission of *The Wall Street Journal* © 1994 Dow Jones & Company, Inc. All rights reserved.

FIRST EDITION

Library of Congress Cataloging-in Publication Data
Frum, David, 1960–
    What's right : the new conservative majority and the remaking of America / David Frum. — 1st ed.
      p.   cm.
    Includes index.
    ISBN 0–465–04197–3
    1. Conservatism—United States.   2. United States—Politics and government—1989–   I. Title.
JC573.2.U6F783   1996
320.5'2'0973—dc20   96-7926

96 97 98 99 00 ❖/HC 10 9 8 7 6 5 4 3 2 1

To Miranda and Nathaniel, who may someday be curious about the passions that roiled their parents' youth.

Contents

PART III
BOOKS AND THINKERS

Acknowledgments

As always, the first word of thanks must go to my wife, Danielle. Every essay in this book has benefited from her wisdom, her kindness, and her faultless editorial eye. I cannot begin to reckon the help and comfort she has given me over nine years of life together. Truly,

> She is mine own,
> And I as rich in having such a jewel
> As twenty seas, if all their sand were pearl,
> The water nectar and the rocks pure gold.

Better than any book, my father's unfailing sense of justice and right has taught me the moral worth of business enterprise. It is to his almost unbelievable generosity that I owe my freedom to speak my mind. My old friend Jonathan Rauch gave me my start in journalism with a column on the editorial page of the *Yale Daily News*. As he is usually the first to point out, it's a favor that's never been adequately repaid. I can't imagine how I could begin to repay William F. Buckley for his innumerable acts of friendship to me; but I remember and am grateful. I am grateful also for the kindnesses shown me by Stewart Pinkerton of *Forbes* and Robert Bartley of the *Wall Street Journal*.

I am deeply indebted, both metaphorically and literally, to Kermit Hummel of Basic Books and Doug Pepper of Random House Canada; whatever hope I have of escaping these debts rests on the spirited and untiring work of my literary agent, Mildred Marmur. The Manhattan Institute, its president, Larry Mone, and its chairman, Roger Hertog, have provided unstinting help for this and other projects. Thank you!

Introduction

Living in the vicinity of intellectual conservatism since the mid-1970s has been very like growing up in one of those amazing Chinese economic zones where placid rice fields have erupted into gigantic cities in barely two decades. Twenty years ago, conservatism was a ghetto ideology. Conservatives wrote for conservative magazines, were published by conservative publishing houses, taught at conservative colleges, and obtained what little airtime they could get on conservative AM radio stations. In the entire country, only two important newspapers—the *Wall Street Journal* and the *Orange County Register*—took a consistently conservative editorial position. On the three great networks, conservative voices were permanently set to "mute."

Yes, in rare cases unusually talented individual conservatives—William F. Buckley, George F. Will—could escape the ghetto and win acclaim in the mainstream. Yes too, neoclassicists had conquered the academic discipline of economics. Yes, finally, by the mid-1970s a small band of writers with preexisting fame, angrily dubbed neoconservatives by their former friends, were already lending strength and prestige to the conservative cause. Even so, a wise adult would in those days have been obliged to recommend an ambitious young person against a career in right-wing journalism. (Certainly the wise adults in my life recommended against it.)

Not for the first time, though, history took a queer bounce. Opinions that looked substantial and sensible in 1975—the wisdom of arms control, the need to strictly control increases in the price of petroleum, the value of psychotherapy—now appear as *démodé* as the era's outlandish clothes and hairstyles. Beliefs once marginal—that the sexual revolution went too far, that affirmative action is a mistake, that taxes impede economic growth—have become, if not quite orthodox, remarkably close to it. This momentous cultural change has been driven by two momentous historical facts: the collapse of communism and the failure of the war on poverty.

At the end of the Cold War, it briefly became conventional to suggest that the jig was now up for conservatism. Without anti-communism, how would this ragtag coalition hold together? The snide implication was that conservatism got its oomph in the same way as a witch doctor in an old B-movie: terrifying its mindless followers by shaking at them a wooden stick with a skull on top. And sure enough, conservatism's internal quarrels have grown angrier and louder since 1989.

But now look at what the collapse of communism has done to conservatism's ideological rivals. Scarcely a month goes by without a revelation from the Soviet archives that corroborates the direst claims of the most virulent Cold Warriors. The Rosenbergs really were guilty; central planning really was an abject economic disaster; the nuclear freeze movement really was subsidized by Moscow; Ronald Reagan's arms buildup really did force the Soviet regime into bankruptcy. Above all, on the two central issues of the Cold War argument at home—Was communism so very dreadful? Was not communism, even if dreadful, something that the West simply had to learn to live with?—the hard-liners have been vindicated and the soft-liners humiliatingly refuted.

The intellectual aftershocks reach beyond foreign policy debates. Communism didn't just collapse—it collapsed for precisely the reason that Ludwig von Mises predicted it would back in 1922: the choking, irrational wastefulness of a planned economy. Without freely moving prices to tell managers the real cost of things, the Soviet economy routinely built machines that were worth less new than they would be if melted down for scrap.

The wreckage of the world's most thoroughly planned economy (Soviet joke: Was socialism invented by scientists or by workers? By workers obviously—scientists would have tested it on hamsters first) has established the free market not merely as the best, but as the only way to organize an economy. Twenty years ago, a Democrat like Jimmy Carter could propose to cope with rising energy prices by inventing a fantastic national system of price controls, rationing, and subsidies. A Republican like Richard Nixon could imagine that inflation could by halted by comprehensive wage and price controls. Who now would take either idea seriously? As a system of social organization, the market no longer faces an intellectually respectable rival.

Of course, it's possible to envisage a market economy with an elaborate welfare state. Prices would move freely, and the government would intervene only to transfer some of their gains from the healthy and the successful to the old, the sick, and the poor. In his later years, John Stuart Mill argued for superimposing just such a system of redistribution on top of a free-market economy. Lyndon Johnson's Great Society attempted to enact something very like it.

Thirty years—and untold billions later—Americans have come to a dismal verdict on Mill's bright idea. Rightly or wrongly, they blame welfare and the welfare state for the havoc in America's cities. Where the American electorate has led, electorates throughout the Western world are following: in Britain, New Zealand, Canada, even continental Europe, citizens have learned from harsh experience that an unconditional promise to aid all in need tends over time to plunge more and more of the population deeper and deeper into dependency and squalor.

A third force, more nebulous than the other two, can also, I believe, be glimpsed behind the rise of the political right over the past two decades. The biggest generation in history is older now. It has married, had children. It's paying taxes and attempting to put money aside for retirement. It's confronting the imminence of death. Those a little younger—beginning with my own cohorts, the class of '82, technically but not emotionally the last bang of the Baby Boom—have grown up in unusually unsettling circumstances, in an economy that offers bigger rewards than ever for the successful, but shrinking rewards for everyone else. Never before has America loomed over the world with such unchallenged military supremacy; seldom have Americans strained more nervously at strange noises in the basement and unexplained groans from the attic. Crime, family disintegration, the decline of educational standards, the deterioration in public decorum, the assault on the worth and importance of America's European cultural inheritance—they don't alarm everyone, but they alarm enough to prepare an unprecedentedly warm welcome for those who ponder these problems and offer substantial solutions for them.

It is as a response both to the discrediting of the liberal alternative and the perception of American decline that political conservatism has triumphed. And in the wake of political conservatism's success, intellectual conservatism has gleefully burst forth from its ghetto. Conservatives now compete on more or less equal terms for national attention: in the publishing houses, in the great newspapers, on television, on the magazine racks. This escape from the margins of political life has, of course, been a magnificent opportunity—but one for which conservatives have not always been fully prepared. We still carry with us the stigmata of our decades in exile: habits of suspicion, of resentment, of conformity. We have not ceased to regard ourselves as primarily an oppositional force.

Now we must. Conservatism used to be a subversive philosophy. Conservatives delighted in mocking their opponents and shattering their preposterous pieties. There's always room for subversiveness in politics. But what conservatism as a movement now needs from its thinkers and writers is *responsibility*: clear-eyed analysis, the digestion of facts, particularly unwelcome facts, and the constant checking of public policies against first principles. I wish I could say that that's what I do; it is, at least, what I try to do.

I have spent most of my adult life watching conservative politics from a series of convenient vantage points. I began fifteen years ago at the *Yale Daily News*. I witnessed the death of socialism in eastern Europe in 1989–1991 from the *Wall Street Journal*'s editorial page. Now I enjoy a ringside view of Washington's endless bouts of mud-wrestling thanks to William Kristol and the *Weekly Standard*. I'm a partisan, and the reader has to make due allowance for that. But I don't believe that partisanship must occlude one's vision. Sometimes it's an intense commitment to a cause that best motivates us to think critically about it.

In one of his essays, George Orwell describes buying a bound volume of magazines from the time of the Napoleonic wars, and marvels how much you can learn about a time from reading its ephemera. Nothing conveys the spirit and passions of an age—sensible or foolish—better than its journalism. The pieces gathered here reflect a half-decade's worth of controversies in the United States and my native country, Canada. They have been altered only to minimize anachronisms. Through them, though, runs one principal theme: the need for conservatives to tread a straight path between a pair of potential dangers—on the one hand, compromising their core value, antistatism, in pursuit of electoral success; on the other, forgetting that conservatism aspires to be a program of government, that it is not merely a style of thought from which to launch a social critique. In its senescence, academic Marxism has adopted a new name for itself—"critical theory"—as if to acknowledge that it no longer has anything positive to suggest about how society might be ordered. Conservatism, though, is not a critical theory. It bristles with plans, policies, and proposals.

Quite rightly too. Plans, policies, and proposals are exactly what the American public demands from would-be leaders. I often wonder about the source of the cliché that Americans are a uniquely optimistic people. This strikes me as the very opposite of the truth. Americans have a vast, insatiable craving for predictions of disaster, be it the Biblical Armageddon, environmental apocalypse, or global financial meltdown. What distinguishes Americans is not their rosy view of the world, but their bottomless faith in the efficacy of action. Whether you are selling thin thighs in thirty days or the Contract with America, you had better offer a ten-point action plan.

But it's also true that intelligent activism must begin with reflection. Conservatism is a philosophy founded on deep convictions about man and society. Conservatives may avoid some unnecessary mistakes if they indulge a little those of us who want to take the time to check our policies against our convictions—even when events are moving at the hyper tempo of Newt Gingrich's Washington. This book is an attempt to suggest how conservatives ought to think. It is divided into three sections: essays about policies, essays about the politicians who execute those policies, and essays about the ideas and convictions from which those policies derive. I hope the title of this book will be understood as a declaration of my aspirations rather than as a boastful self-appraisal of the merits of the work gathered here. Thinking hard, thinking rightly, is a duty as onerous as any that the public has entrusted to the Republican politicians of the 104th Congress. It's a duty that Republican success has now imposed on an entire generation of conservative writers.

PART I

Politics and Politicians

Who Is Newt Gingrich?

Is Newt Gingrich a joke?

A strange question to ask about the man currently in effective control of the government of the United States. But Newt Gingrich has long invited mockery. His overheated rhetorical style (he never merely "learns" or "discovers" something: he is "shocked to learn" or "stunned to discover"), his fondness for sweeping historical analogies, his susceptibility to self-improvement gurus and glib futurists—these quirks have been eliciting giggles from congressional reporters since Gingrich arrived on Capitol Hill in 1979. The release of an early draft of Gingrich's novel *1945*, featuring a German sex kitten spy amok in wartime Washington, did not win Gingrich any new reputation for gravitas either. The witty *New York Times* columnist Maureen Dowd has quipped that Gingrich's most characteristic expression is that of a four-year-old who has just deliberately smeared his face with chocolate pudding.

But of course, Gingrich is not a joke. He is not merely an operator either, although that's the way Washingtonians think of him on those occasions that they decide to take him seriously. When his literary agent first proposed to gather into a book a course of lectures Gingrich had delivered over the past five years at two small colleges in Georgia, the idea was news not for the literary pages but for Washington's tireless ethics cops. Gingrich's $4.5 million advance from HarperCollins* was widely attacked as little more than a bribe from Rupert Murdoch, HarperCollins's owner. Adverse publicity forced Gingrich to drop the advance and to wait for royalties—which seem to be flowing in abundance. But the

*Which happens to be the parent company of Basic Books.

early flap persuaded journalists in the capital that they need pay little attention to the book's actual contents. Michael Kinsley, the
astringent liberal commentator, insisted in the *New Republic* that
even to write a hostile review of *To Renew America* was to fall into
Gingrich's trap.

What Gingrich is—and what he should be understood as—is
the architect of the startling political upset of 1994. It was Gingrich
who identified corruption and arrogance as the themes that could
bring to an end the Democrats' forty-year lock on the House of
Representatives; Gingrich who maneuvered the Democrats into
opposing term limits on Congress while deftly avoiding any
Republican commitment to support them; Gingrich who goaded
the Democrats into breaking with the strategy that had preserved
their power since the late 1970s—keeping congressional elections
focused upon local issues—and into the disastrous strategy of fight-
ing a broad, national, ideological campaign.

Nor has Gingrich faltered since. Not for a generation has the
majority party in Congress passed a coherent program of legislation. But under Gingrich's leadership, the new Republican majority
in the House is firing off enactment after enactment with hardly a
dissenting vote, while the shattered Democrats turn their anger on
one another. Gingrich must be reckoned the most effective leader
of Congress since Lyndon Johnson's departure from the Senate in
1961—and as the true leader of the Republican party nationally. If
the Republicans choose the uninspiring Robert Dole as their nominee for president in 1996, they will only further consolidate the
dominance of the dynamic Gingrich over the party.

So while it is true that *To Renew America* shows the seams and
joins where it was spliced together out of speeches, tape-recorded
reminiscences, off-the-top-of-the-head opinions, and memoranda
by aides—while it will certainly never rank among the classics of
political literature—it's a book that students of American politics
will want to pay close attention to. *To Renew America* isn't so much
a book to be read, as a document to be analyzed. The fact that it
was written by others does not prevent it from telling us a very
great deal about its putative author.

To Renew America is a book of lists. On pages 33 and 34, we
find the "five basic principles that I believe form the heart of our
civilization." Later, Gingrich ticks off "the eight major changes
which need to be undertaken simultaneously" to open opportunities for the poor, the "five major distinctions between Second and

Third Wave education," the three imminent revolutions in health care, the nine steps that must be taken right now to improve health standards, and so on. It's a technique that Gingrich has borrowed from self-help books and women's magazines: *the nine things you must do NOW to win financial independence; six things every woman must know about men; ten steps you can take today to help your child at math.* But then that's the point. Books and magazines that offer ten-point programs sell. They appeal to the profound American faith in action and the resolvability of all difficulties, no matter how intractable they might seem.

Despite Americans' much-advertised loss of faith in government, this problem-solving spirit still animates the political world. Nobody ever got elected to anything by saying, "There is no political solution to the problem of"—fill in the blank. "Government can only make matters worse. I therefore propose to do nothing."

Americans want action from their politicians, and politicians, emphatically including conservative politicians, therefore want to take action. And action (or the appearance of it) is a Gingrich specialty. To read Gingrich—and, even more, to talk to him—is to be plunged into a frenzy of motion, a whirl of activity. You hear truths that *will frankly shock* you, that prove that American civilization stands *on the brink* of renewal or decay, unless we together take the following five steps *right now*.

As a method of understanding the external world, the Gingrich method may lack rigor. But as a method of motivating followers it cannot be improved on. The Gingrich enthusiasm jolted the demoralized Republican congressional party of the late 1970s, headed by unimaginative leaders interested only in cutting personal deals to benefit their own districts. Gingrich infuses every issue he takes on with the thrilling atmosphere of world history. When he compares the work of the 104th Congress to the progress of Wellington in the Peninsular Campaign, he is not essaying a precise analogy, nor is he crudely showing off his erudition. He is instead making a claim about the immense importance of the work his party is doing—and pointedly reminding his followers that it is his own genius for mythmaking that can persuade the public to see that work's importance.

Modern congressional leaders possess nothing like the arsenal of weapons that Speakers and Senate Majority Leaders deployed in the 1950s and 1960s. Today's Speaker holds his authority on exactly the same terms as the old kings of Aragon, to whom their barons pledged fealty with the uncomfortable oath: "We, who are no worse than you, pledge to you, who are no better than we, to follow you so long as you obey our laws—and if not, not." Yes, Gingrich's political action committee can raise money and distribute it to promising freshmen. Yes too, he holds sway over committee assignments. But really his power rests on his ability to mobilize his congressional caucus.

Interpreted that way, the peculiarities of *To Renew America* suddenly make a great deal of sense. To party conservatives worried about America's moral decay, Gingrich offers a diagnosis of the country's ailments as sweeping and apocalyptic as their own. "We are certainly not the first civilization to confront moral decay from within. But we are definitely *the first generation in American history* to face such a challenge" (italics in original). For party moderates disturbed by the potentially excessive implications of this dire assessment, Gingrich offers an alternative diagnosis, one that attributes the country's stresses and turmoil to the pace of technological change. "If people become overwhelmed with change, said [Alvin and Heidi Toffler], they could go into a state of dejection and exhaustion. . . . [T]he transformation we are experiencing is so large and historic that it can be compared with only two other great eras of human history—the Agricultural Revolution and the Industrial Revolution."

Gingrich's notorious technospeak is not babble, or anyway not merely babble. It cleverly bridges a real political chasm. And this is the authentic Gingrich method. He effortlessly moves back and forth between radical diagnosis and mild prescription. Here's Gingrich on education, for example: "Americans now face an unprecedented learning crisis. . . . Our failing is that we keep seeking *education* rather than *learning*. We invest more time and money in an old industrial–era, Second Wave school system" (italics in original). How can this frighteningly antiquated system be modernized? Gingrich proposes to pay poor children a cash prize for every book they read, to promote the use of computers in the early grades, to accelerate promotion out of high school, and to encourage adults to take continuing education courses after the end of formal schooling. Interesting ideas, and possibly meritorious, but hardly amounting to a "Third Wave Information Age learning system that is as different from the current bureaucratic model as the space shuttle is from an 1845 stage coach." In a party bitterly divided between reforming Republicans who want to reinvent the schools and suburban Republicans whose constituents like their schools just the way they are and suspect that reform will result only in compulsory sharing of those schools with rougher children from the wrong side of the tracks, the discrepancy between the two halves of Gingrich's approach to the education problem strikes exactly the correct political balance.

Of course, the congressional caucus is not Gingrich's only constituency. It is no secret that Gingrich intends some day to run for president. *To Renew America* tells us a great deal about how he plans to do it. While the book revels in futuristic visions, its tone has clearly been influenced by the effusive New Age style of President Clinton. Events are always described in terms of their emotional impact upon Gingrich. "One incident in Douglasville, Georgia, turned me into a revolutionary." "The whole scene gave me a wonderful sense of the romance of America." "When I look at my daughters and their husbands, my nieces and nephews, I know I'm willing to go a long way to protect them." "My interest in the environment goes back to my childhood." "At heart, I am still a happy four-year-old who gets up every morning hoping to find a cookie that friends or relatives may have left for me somewhere."

American politics will no longer tolerate the emotional austerity of a Robert Taft or the amused aloofness of an Adlai Stevenson. Newt—we are all on a first-name basis with him—understands the sentimentality of the political culture in which he operates. It is not enough to tell an affecting story; you must describe how you were affected by it. It is not enough to be right; you must also be lovable.

Ironically enough, Gingrich's most attractive feature is how resolutely unlovable he remains. A tough operator, a master of the workings of modern representative politics, a man of ideas and a subversively high level of culture—that's Gingrich. He is not a man to make Bill Clinton's mistake of confusing feeling with doing. Which is why, unlike his soon-to-be-utterly-forgotten Clinton, Newt Gingrich—at whichever end of Pennsylvania Avenue he resides—is poised to dominate American politics for a generation.

The Elite Primary

Think of the Democratic Party as a particularly wild debutante. Again and again she ignores the tut-tutting of her friends and hurls herself at some mysterious stranger: JFK, McGovern, Carter, Dukakis, Clinton. Think of the Republican Party as the Democrats' serious-minded sister. In all but one of the past nine elections she has opted for her highest-ranking or most senior leader: Nixon in 1960, 1968, and 1972; Ford, Reagan, Reagan, Bush, Bush. To find an election in which the party rejected its heir apparent in favor of an insurgent, one has to look all the way back to 1964, when the draft-Goldwater movement knocked aside Nelson Rockefeller, the multi-millionaire governor of New York State.

In the fall of 1995, three men—Phil Gramm, Pete Wilson, and Lamar Alexander—entertained serious hopes of besting 1996's Republican heir apparent, Bob Dole. Gramm and Wilson could at least claim some heir-apparent legitimacy of their own—Gramm as the Senate's Mr. Conservative, Wilson as the governor of the largest state in the nation. Lamar Alexander, however, stood way, way back in the Republican queue. His résumé (two-term governor of Tennessee, Secretary of Education under George Bush), while creditable, ought to have pushed him down among the Dick Lugars and Arlen Specters, and other no-hopers. But for all his lack of reputation, Alexander persisted.

By the end of the June 1996 Federal Elections Commission filing period, he had raised $7.6 million—less than Bob Dole's $13.4 million, but a considerable amount of money by anybody's definition. Six of the past eight Republican National Committee finance chairmen joined his campaign. Alexander signed up the most brilliant of Republican media men, Mike Murphy, some of the cleverest of the Washington policy works, Pete Wilson's onetime biggest donor, and the man who chaired Bob Dole's 1988 New Hampshire

9

campaign. Alexander's strategists insisted that it was precisely because their man was *not* the heir apparent that he could incarnate the populist anti-Washington political passions of the 1990s. They intended, they said, to run an insurgency campaign, very like the campaigns that nominated Barry Goldwater in 1964 and Jimmy Carter in 1976 and that nearly nominated Gary Hart in 1984.

But there remained one difference: the Goldwater, Carter, and Hart campaigns drew their strength from the enthusiasm of previously disorganized voting blocs. Goldwater excited the nascent conservative movement, Carter mobilized evangelical voters, and Hart appealed to upper-income Democrats who leaned to the right of their party economically and to the left of it on social issues. It was not, however, *voter* excitement that fueled the Alexander campaign. Alexander boasted nothing like the network of militants who seized the Republican nomination for Goldwater. His campaign was a phalanx of Republican donors and campaign operatives—an army of generals and colonels. For all Alexander's attacks on out-of-touch political elites, it's hard to remember a Republican candidacy that gambled so completely on the power and persuasiveness of those same elites. And Alexander's ability to persist in the contest with hardly any popular support—to go on paying the exorbitant costs of a first-tier presidential campaign despite his prolonged 4-percent showing in the polls—demonstrated that the gamble was not an entirely misconceived one.

In an excess of irony, twenty years of political reforms intended to minimize the influence of wealthy donors and maximize popular participation in the nominating process have achieved precisely the opposite result. Increasingly, the crucial primary does not occur in any one particular state: it is a shadowy national competition to raise money, sign up prominent supporters, and impress the media in the year preceding the election year. It is this "elite primary" that winnowed out Jack Kemp, Dick Cheney, and other Republican aspirants.

The more ingenious Alexander, in contrast, brilliantly turned the system to his own advantage. The Tennessee law firm of former Senator Howard Baker cheerfully payed Alexander a salary of $295,000 for the services he could spare it in the intervals between full-time campaigning. (That sum lands with a gratifying smack atop the $3 million to $6 million fortune that—as Lisa Schiffren reported in the September 1995 *American Spectator*—generous friends helped Alexander accumulate with hardly any money down.) And it was his success in the elite primary that marked Lamar Alexander as a serious candidate in 1996, despite his near-total prior invisibility among the Republican rank and file.

Materialist explanations of history have, for obvious reasons, fallen out of fashion recently. Nevertheless, it is two hard material facts that shape the system of presidential-candidate selection: the primary schedule and the campaign-finance laws.

As late as 1968 fewer than half the voting delegates at the national party conventions were chosen by primary voters. That year Robert F. Kennedy won every primary he entered except Oregon's, but had he lived he almost certainly would have lost the Democratic nomination to the favorite of the party leaders, Vice President Hubert Humphrey.

Selection by party leaders was not to happen again. The late 1960s and early 1970s were a time of immense suspicion of traditional elites and hierarchies, and in those years state after state abandoned the old caucus and convention methods of delegate selection in favor of the primary. By 1972 a majority of those able to cast a ballot at a national convention had been elected in a state primary and arrived pledged to a candidate. But the two parties did not immediately digest the logic of the primary system. For years it appeared that little had changed. The nomination fight proceeded at the leisurely pace of the early years of the century, beginning in Iowa in the dead of winter, arriving in the big midwestern states in the spring, and culminating in California in early June.

The first candidate to understand the implications of imposing a new method of picking delegates upon the old schedule was Jimmy Carter. He realized that by painstakingly working the state of Iowa for months, almost as if he were running for governor, he could post a surprisingly strong showing in its caucases. His win in Iowa transformed him into a national figure, enabling him to raise money to fight the big, costly primaries later in the year. George Bush copied the Carter method in 1980, and though he didn't win the Republican nomination, he did promote himself from being a relatively inconsequential politician into the vice presidency.

But the Carter method hasn't worked since. In the mid-1980s the leisurely schedule inherited from the bygone days of caucuses and state conventions began to be compressed. Anxious to pull their party in a more conservative direction, southern Democrats grouped their 1988 primaries together in one "Super Tuesday." With hundreds of delegates from the nation's most conservative states up for grabs on a single day in March, relatively early in the primary season, aspirants would, it was hoped, adopt a new, right-leaning political argot. At first the plan backfired—with Richard Gephardt, Al Gore, and Michael Dukakis dividing the white vote, the surprise beneficiary of the first Super Tuesday was Jesse Jackson—but it did succeed in cramping the hopes of Carter-style insurgents by denying them time to capitalize on early successes in the small states. In 1988 Bob Dole and Pat Robertson relegated George Bush to a humiliating third-place finish in Iowa, to no avail. In 1992 Pat Buchanan's primary challenge to President Bush soon fizzled out, despite an impressive 37-percent finish in New Hampshire.

It is only in the past two years, however, that the primary system has reached its full logical conclusion. Why, state party officials in places like Arizona and Delaware wondered, should Iowa and New Hampshire call the tune? *We want to be relevant.* And why, officeholders in giant states like California and Ohio asked in their turn, should dinky states like Arizona and Delaware take control of the nomination from Iowa and New Hampshire? *We want to be relevant too.* And so was triggered a pell-mell scramble forward through the calendar.

In 1992, despite Super Tuesday, it took the Republicans until April 27 to nominate 60 percent of their delegates, and until May 5—the old date of the Ohio primary—to get past 70 percent. In 1996 nearly 70 percent of all Republican delegates were chosen by April Fool's Day. Before, a losing candidate might keep struggling, hoping to pick up some of California's huge block of delegates in the first week of June. California now votes at the end of March, and after that a trailing candidate is definitively out of the race.

The intensification of the schedule does not merely speed up the nominating process; it also spreads it out geographically. A candidate must now campaign in more states at the same time than ever before: Colorado and Connecticut, Georgia and Maine, Maryland and Massachusetts, Minnesota, Rhode Island, and Vermont, all voted on March 5 in 1996, and New York on March 7. Texas and Oregon, Florida and Mississippi, Tennessee and Oklahoma voted a week later. Jimmy Carter enjoyed seven weeks of relative calm in which to fund-raise after Iowa in 1976. In 1996 candidates needed to charter jets, gear up national organizations, and buy Atlanta, Los Angeles, and New York City broadcast time as early as mid-February. They needed to have their millions banked by

Christmas—or even earlier. Even in New Hampshire, television commercials have become decisive. David Shribman, the Pulitzer Prize–winning Washington bureau chief of the *Boston Globe,* has covered New Hampshire primaries for twenty years. He says it has long since ceased to be true that you can carry New Hampshire by shaking hands: "You can't win if you're on the village green but not on the television screen."

Which bumps us up against the other hard fact of American politics: its campaign-finance laws. These laws, adopted in the wake of the Watergate scandal, set a $1,000 maximum on any individual's gift to a presidential candidate and a $5,000 maximum on giving by a political-action committee. They also effectively imposed a cap on what a presidential candidate who accepts federal matching funds may spend to win the nomination—in 1996, about $36 million. In one of politics' most spectacular examples of the Law of Unintended Consequences, the Democratic authors of the reforms, who hoped to limit the influence of the wealthy on the presidential race and at the same time to enhance the relative clout of their trade-union allies (labor unions' PACs at the time were more powerful than they are now), instead enlarged the power of contributors beyond all previous measure.

In unreformed America a candidate like George McGovern could run for office with the support of a few very rich backers who held eccentric ideas. But with an individual-donor limit of $1,000 and a spending limit of $36 million, it no longer suffices to locate a few eccentric millionaires. A candidate must spend the now-all-important year before the primaries winning the support of thousands of affluent contributors. It's like filling a bathtub with a tablespoon. And since not even the most grimly determined candidate can woo so many people one by one, he or she must first win the support of the few hundred maestros of the Rolodex who have proved their ability and willingness to sponsor the fund-raising galas, cocktail parties, breakfast meetings, and intimate suppers necessary to extract the requisite quota of funds from each major region's check-writing Democrats and Republicans. What campaign-finance reform has done is to take a commodity in which America rolls in ridiculous oversupply, money, and create an artificial shortage of it—and thus an artificial inflation of the influence and power of those who can mobilize it.

The wooing of these money mobilizers has, then, become one of the essential first steps of modern campaigning. The pursuit of

Cheney moneyman Mel Sembler, a Florida developer and Bush-appointed ambassador to Australia, was a contest as avidly fought and as important as any early caucus or straw-poll beauty contest. (In the end Sembler threw himself behind Alexander.) In his remarkable book *The United States of Ambition,* Alan Ehrenhalt observes that the old mechanisms for screening candidates have collapsed, and that candidates—once nominated by parties—now nominate themselves. At the presidential level, at least, that isn't quite true: the party bosses may have vanished, but in their place we have the Rolodex men, and behind them the press.

Compare Alexander with another Republican presidential aspirant—Carroll Campbell of South Carolina. Like Alexander, Campbell was twice elected governor of a traditionally Democratic southern state. Like Alexander's, Campbell's tenure was widely regarded as an immense success: he modernized South Carolina's antique government by shearing the powers of the state's largely unsupervised boards, agencies, and commissions and enhancing the more accountable office of the governor. He worked for education reform, kept the state's books in good order, and cut taxes. He deftly combined political conservatism with racial moderation. He even lured a car maker, BMW, to the state. When George Bush lost in 1992, Campbell too began to plan a run for the presidency. He believed that a win in the early South Carolina primary could propel a popular governor to national prominence. Campbell had lined up the support of financial contributors and some of his fellow governors. But as state after state brought its primary forward, Campbell's hopes faded.

"They changed the ball game," he says. "The whole ball game. We figured we'd probably be good for five or six million dollars. Under the old route I would have run in Iowa, New Hampshire, and South Carolina and then gone into Little Tuesday. That was the old route: I had a chance to run, raise money as I went, and have a decent showing along the way.

"Now you've no time to raise money as you go. There's no time to do your mailings and get it back in and keep up the cash flow. You have to run in all the big states at the same time, which is an impossibility for a candidate who is not extremely well known or extremely well funded.

"I had a group of people in New Jersey and some in New York who were raising money. I had some people in Texas, and I had a good group in California. But they couldn't raise the huge amounts because of the [per-contributor] limitations. I had people who could have raised enough money or given individually if they could have given at a higher level. You're not raising money with a tablespoon; it's more like a teaspoon when it's compared with the amount of money you're going to spend."

Today Campbell gloomily occupies the presidency of the insurance industry's lobbying organization.

What's the difference between Alexander and Campbell? To a considerable extent it's Ted Welch, a former Republican national-finance chairman and Alexander's principal Rolodex man. Welch had success publishing Bibles, dictionaries, and cookbooks, and then heaped up a larger fortune with lucrative real-estate ventures in Nashville. He has known Alexander for nearly a quarter of a century, and began discussing a run for the presidency with him as early as 1982. Welch picked me up one Sunday evening at the Stouffer Hotel in Nashville—a hotel he built in a downtown complex he developed—dressed in an expensive blazer over a sport shirt. As we drove off, he picked up his car phone, telephoned the restaurant he'd chosen, and said with the guiltless gusto of the Sunbelt rich: "This is Ted Welch calling. Your landlord. Can we have a quiet booth at the back?"

Over a pizza he explained how his job is done. "I don't call strictly out of the blue. I'll have some reason to believe that he is either for or susceptible to being for Alexander. One of Lamar's main fund-raisers in Florida has never raised money before. Lamar taught her canoeing at an exclusive camp in Florida when Lamar was seventeen and this lady was thirteen. She happened to be a friend of mine to begin with. And she's become a very enthusiastic fund-raiser."

This reliance on friendships was typical of the Alexander campaign. Alexander's supporters seem not only to be uninterested in his message but to be actively disregarding it. A moderate as governor and Education secretary (although he prefers the term "activist conservative"), since the summer of 1993 Alexander has been seeking the presidency as an ultra-Jeffersonian radical. "The principal threat to freedom abroad has collapsed," he says, "but the principal threat at home has grown more menacing. The evil empire in the Kremlin has been defeated, spreading freedom in its wake. But the government in Washington, D.C., has become an arrogant

empire, spreading its tentacles into our everyday lives." To combat
the arrogance of Washington, he has proposed radical reform of
Congress: "Cut their pay and send them home. Cut in half the
time Congress spends in Washington. Cut their pay in half. Take
off the rules that prohibit their taking a real job, and let them work
alongside the rest of us." He calls for a major devolution of responsibility from Washington to the states, ending the role of the federal
government in welfare, crime control, and education.

Strong stuff. Yet the Republicans applauding it seem to be
drawn almost exclusively from the ideological left of the Republican Party. Tom Rath, Alexander's genial New Hampshire campaign chairman, voted for Gerald Ford over Ronald Reagan in the
1976 New Hampshire primary and for Howard Baker in 1980, and
worked for Bob Dole in 1988. Bill Cahill, Alexander's New Hampshire campaign director, was communications director for Vice
President Bush's New Hampshire primary campaign in 1988.
David Wilson, one of the wealthiest men in Tennessee and an
Alexander donor for many years, supported Bush over Reagan in
1980.

To be sure, when asked, Alexander can tick off the names of
supporters who hail from more-conservative precincts. Indeed, his
communications director last worked for Oliver North. But anyone
who has hung around the conservative movement and the Republican Party need only walk into Alexander's campaign office on
Nashville's West End Avenue to recognize instantly the atmosphere
of Republican centrism: the attractive, well-groomed young volun-
teers, the avoidance of hard-edged issues, the way words like
"process" and "consensus" trip off tongues. "Lamar Alexander is a
Howard Baker protégé through and through," says his longtime
friend M. Lee Smith, now the owner of a company that publishes
legal newsletters. (Baker, of course, incarnated middle-of-the-road
Republicanism.) "Lamar is not a hard-core conservative. He has
adopted a lot more conservative rhetoric in this campaign, I guess
in part because the country is moving in that direction and the
party especially has."

Alexander himself avoids overtly ideological discourse. "I'm not
running for senator, and I'm not running for think-tank president.
I'm running for chief executive, and what you want in a chief executive to begin with is character and temperament and the ability to
make executive decisions." Unfortunately for him, that's not what
the secular and religious conservatives who form the only potential

base of support for a challenge to Bob Dole want. They want some confidence that a candidate not only can make decisions but will make decisions congenial to them. And whether or not they feel that confidence depends on an elite that operates alongside the Rolodex men: the press.

In the past the press has mattered far more to Democratic candidates than to Republicans—in part because the Republican nominee was usually marked out so early, in part because Republicans have mistrusted the reporting of what they see as the overwhelmingly liberal media. A sympathetic press helped Bill Clinton to regain his lead after Paul Tsongas won the New Hampshire primary in 1992. Joe Klein, who wrote a cover story for *New York* magazine that is sometimes credited with attracting the city's big Democratic donors to Clinton, recalls that "it was just obvious" that Clinton was the best candidate in the Democratic field—which is, he hastily adds, as much a comment on that field as on Bill Clinton. But Clinton's superiority to Bob Kerrey and Paul Tsongas might not have been so obvious to voters who had not invested the time to learn of the former's flakiness and the latter's health troubles. The consensus on Clinton, Klein recalls, was the product of the reporting of journalists, the buzzing of party people and consultants, and the preferences of Democratic check writers in Chicago, New York, and Los Angeles.

Now there have emerged explicitly Republican media to do for that party the same sorting long done for Democrats by the tacitly Democratic networks and major metropolitan papers; magazines like the *American Spectator, National Review,* and the new *Weekly Standard,* the editorial page of the *Wall Street Journal,* and—maybe above all—Rush Limbaugh. When Alexander backers meet skepticism toward their claim that their candidate is the most conservative in the race, they fall back on the argument that he is "sufficiently" conservative. Should the Alexander campaign show signs of succeeding, the credibility of that claim among Republican primary voters will depend to quite an amazing extent on whether Limbaugh and the conservative press buy it.

Is this bad? Is it wrong that relatively small groups of people should have arrogated to themselves the task of promoting potential presidents, as Ted Welch has done, or vetoing them, as the press has the power to do? The rhetoric of American democracy insists that it is wrong. Even Lamar Alexander—whose candidacy exists only and entirely because of his skill at exciting the enthusiasm of Republican organizers—takes pains to present himself as an opponent of elites. Hence the trademark red-and-black-checked shirt.

But let's entertain for a moment a heretical thought. If not for the Ted Welches, how could American democracy work? This is an enormous country, and virtually everybody in it has work to do and children to raise. Once upon a time the machinery of the two great political parties sorted through the potential candidates. But that machinery rusted away long ago. All that remains is the candidates themselves, a hundred million voters unwilling to contribute very much more to the political process than their ballot on Election Day, and, interceding between them, some tens of thousands of donors, party activists, political professionals, and journalists. Some utopian political theorists imagine that if it were not for this group of intercessors, American democracy would revert to the intensely participatory politics of the earliest days of the Republic. Fat chance. In an era of immense wealth and instant communications, a politics somehow liberated from the political class—if such a thing can be imagined at all—would resemble the Jesse Jackson campaigns of 1984 and 1988 and the Ross Perot campaign of 1992: ad hoc mass movements in the service of charismatic leaders.

As a country imbued with a deep ethic of social equality, America has never reconciled itself to the existence of elites. Elites that frankly acknowledge their own existence and attempt to justify their own position—the Federalist leaders of the 1780s, the new industrial millionaires of the turn of the century—have without exception brought retribution crashing down upon their heads. But the country's anti-elitism has never succeeded in replacing elites with direct popular government, both for the reason identified by James Madison and Alexander Hamilton two centuries ago—the country is too big—and for the reason spelled out by Joseph Schumpeter in the 1940s: the job is too difficult.

Instead, American anti-elitism has again and again replaced explicit elites with disguised ones. Ambitious state-chartered bankers and hungry land speculators in New York exploited anti-elitist feeling to topple the too restrictive Bank of the United States in the 1830s; the Harvard-educated New Dealers appealed to that same emotion to expand the power of people like themselves over the American economy. The populist electoral reforms of that 1960s and 1970s replicated the inevitable pattern. The power to make and unmake presidential candidates has migrated from ward bosses in derby hats and checked suits to local business leaders who can fill a hotel ballroom with friends with checkbooks.

Some may be tempted to adventure yet another round of political reform: full public funding of campaigns or free television advertising. But somebody will still have to decide whether Robert Dornan and Lenora Fulani get money and free television, and how much Bob Dole and Bill Clinton get. The problem of unequal impact on the political system—if it is a problem at all—is simply an ineradicable one.

Maybe there's another way to think about this. Maybe we should be worrying less about the existence of elites and more about their quality, less about their excess of money and more about their deficiencies of public spirit. Maybe we should worry that American society's primordial hostility to elites, its determination to force those elites to disguise themselves and deny their inevitable influence, nourishes their irresponsibility and stunts their sense of public obligation. Maybe we should accept as inevitable that those who care the most about politics can most effectively sway the political system, and should worry instead that this political elite itself is so easily swayed by charm and a home-state accent.

The Powell
Phenomenon

General Powell ran his presidential campaign exactly as he would have liked to have run the Gulf War: a massive buildup of force culminating in a strategic withdrawal. He left stranded behind him what remains of America's centrist establishment—which had invested in the general the hopes so bitterly disappointed by President Clinton—and an assortment of conservatives who, breaking ranks with their fellows, had declared qualified backing for him.

The centrists' enthusiasm for Powell needs no explanation. For them, he was perfect: conservative in tone, liberal in content; a complete creature of Washington; a man who saw the world precisely the way they did. But why conservatives should have backed Powell was something more of a mystery.

Some of Powell's conservative sympathizers argued from tactics. Neither Bob Dole nor Phil Gramm, they reasoned, was likely to succeed in defeating President Clinton in 1996; Colin Powell probably could; therefore, let us overcome our mistrust of him, secure in the confidence that no matter who occupies the White House, a conservative Congress led by Newt Gingrich would do the real work of governing. Other conservatives, conceding the harm that a President Powell might do the conservative cause, declared their support for him anyway, on the grounds that his election would salve America's festering racial troubles. As Charles Krauthammer wrote in October 1995, "For such a man to win the presidency would have a transforming effect on Americans' view of racial possibilities."

Both lines of reasoning were open to question. If Republicans really were thinking of governing from Capitol Hill after 1996, would they not have been better off facing a moderate-to-liberal White House under the leadership of a vacillating and weak Bill Clinton than a moderate-to-liberal White House under the leadership of a strong and hugely popular Colin Powell? Worse, as a nominal Republican, a President Powell would command vastly more deference from the Republican congressional leadership than President Clinton.

As for the argument from racial harmony, its premises seemed equally dubious. Powell's exploration of a presidential run ignited curiously little enthusiasm among black Americans. Perhaps that is because the message conveyed by his career—that blacks who play by the majority's rules can win some very big prizes—is hardly news. Business leaders, police chiefs, clergymen, university presidents, Supreme Court justices, and politicians by the dozens have repeatedly demonstrated this truth, without palliating America's racial conflicts.

If all the reasons given were unconvincing, what made the conservatives' flirtation with Powell all the more puzzling was that their candidate was no Cincinnatus. Had Colin Powell been elected president of the United States, his victory would have lifted out of the humiliating margins of American history a long-despised minority group: staff officers. Every previous general to win the White House has led American troops to victory in combat. Not General Powell; he served two stints in Vietnam, one as an adviser to South Vietnamese troops, and then seven years later as a divisional planning officer. The remainder of his 35-year military career was spent behind a desk.

Nothing wrong with that, of course. The generals who plan operations are every bit as indispensable to military success as the George Pattons and Creighton Abramses. Good staff work can do what the brave-but-stupid William Westmoreland never did: win wars. Even so, desk generals—no matter how capable—have seldom excited much public enthusiasm. It was Ulysses S. Grant rather than Henry Halleck who swept into office in 1868; Dwight Eisenhower, not George C. Marshall, who galvanized the country in 1952. Indisputably, though, Colin Powell does generate excitement. Why?

Powell's boosters lauded his dignity and integrity, and it is certainly true that he exudes a manliness and self-restraint anachronistic in an age of sentimentality and hucksterism. His best-selling autobiography tells a remarkable story. Powell personally transcended racial divisions, and rose to the top of his beloved U.S. Army and by helping it to overcome those same divisions as an institution. When he reached the chairmanship of the Joint Chiefs of Staff, he demonstrated in the most spectacular possible way that he owed his position to outstanding personal merit by bringing the nation its first unequivocal battlefield triumph since 1945.

Yet this argument from character also failed as a justification of Powell's candidacy, for it severed the character of the man from the record of his career. It is a curious fact about Powell's account of himself that he seems far more eager to escape than to claim responsibility for his actions.

At times, this habit seems no more than a defensive verbal tic, as if to ward off an accusation that no one has leveled against him. At other times, something more complicated seems to be going on. Thus, during the investigation of the My Lai massacre perpetrated by the division to which Powell was assigned as planning officer in 1969: "He [the investigator] then asked me if I was custodian of the division's operational journals, and I said I was. He asked me to produce the journal for March 1968. I explained that I had not been with the division at that time."

At the botched invasion of Grenada: "Relations between the services were marred by poor communications, fractured command and control, interservice parochialism, and micromanagement from Washington. . . . I was only a fly on the wall at the time . . . "

When the Iran-Contra scheme was launched: "I had known for months that the arms plan was kicking around. But it was not until the moment that Weinberger directed me to carry out the transfer [of antitank weapons to Iran] that I knew the president had definitely decided to go ahead with it. . . . I decided that the course of wisdom was to draft a memo of my own to Poindexter repeating the legal requirement that Congress must be notified. . . . What we did not know was that Poindexter and company did plan to notify Congress—in the last week of the Reagan administration, three years off."

And when the Clinton administration decided not to send the tanks to Somalia that might have protected the eighteen soldiers killed in Mogadishu in September 1993: "With only three days left in my term, I was in Les Aspin's office making one last pitch to him to give [Gen.] Tom Montgomery the armor he wanted. 'It ain't gonna happen,' Aspin, the political realist, said. . . . I had done what I had to do, a soldier backing soldiers."

Artful silences like these undergirded Powell's military career. They also formed the basis of his (so far abortive) political career. At nearly sixty years of age, and after a decade and a half of service at the very center of America's political system, it did not embarrass him to claim that he was only beginning to evolve a political philosophy. The same man who told us in *My American Journey* that he was neither for nor against sanctions on Saddam Hussein was neither for nor against abortion, neither for nor against gun control, neither for nor against affirmative action.

The case for Powell as presidential candidate was that he was a leader, but where did he want to go? Perhaps he himself did not know. Perhaps, as cautious in peace as in war, he intended to wait for signals from others. Had he not declined to run, the only way to find out would have been to elect him president first.

This "trust me" style of leadership obviously appeals to some deep yearning in American voters. The past two decades of highly charged politics have demanded from ordinary citizens uncomfortable amounts of effort, attention, and tolerance for conflict. It's easy to forget the bitter political quarrels of past generations, and to remember a gentle past, untroubled by rancor and division. Again and again, political leaders have promised to "bring us together" (Richard Nixon's campaign slogan in 1968): to bury the necessity of political choice under a smooth carpet of soothing words.

And so one heard, in the fervent declarations of faith in Powell from the men and women who queued up to have him sign their books, a very understandable desperation to escape the clamor and din of contemporary politics. They seemed to be saying: stop forcing on us these harsh alternatives—banning or funding abortion; cutting or increasing welfare budgets; racial quotas or strict formal equality. Find some sensible middle course that will appeal to everyone, that will unite Americans as (in memory) they were united a generation ago.

In 1992, the candidate who attempted to exploit this sentiment was Ross Perot. Needless to say, Colin Powell is a vastly more admirable man than the opportunistic and sinister Perot. But the appeal itself is based on an illusion—that someone, somehow, can write all of America's contending factions into one post-ideological synthesis—and on a disturbingly widespread popular wish to be relieved of responsibility for the choices the country needs to make.

Which brings us back to the conservatives. What made their differential treatment of Powell all the more striking is that it occurred barely months after Newt Gingrich had proven the extraordinary potential of an entirely different style of politics. The most remarkable thing about the Contract with America—far more remarkable than its contents—was the respect it accorded the electorate: "Here is what we propose to do if entrusted with power. Do you approve or disapprove?" More so than in any congressional election since 1980, or perhaps since 1946, the voters of 1994 knew in advance what their decision at the ballot box would mean. Quite unlike their opponents—who campaigned on the theme, "trust us to know what's best for you"—the Republicans were seeking a mandate for a program, spelled out in advance.

Yet no more than anyone else are conservatives immune to the blandishments of irresponsibility. There is a historical pattern at work here. After a conservative electoral victory, it usually does not take very long before the nerve of some conservative leaders—and followers—fails. It happened after 1968 and again after 1980. The Powell boomlet was a sign that it could be happening again after 1994.

As they survey the arduous legislative program to which the congressional Republican party has committed itself, some conservatives feel their stomachs flutter. Instead of hacking away at the federal government, upsetting the old people and taking risks with the party's popularity, why not (they ask) make it a top priority to elect a Republican president who personifies the right sort of *values*?

In particular, there hovers about some conservatives the desire that national politics be not about governing ("mere budget-balancing") but about teaching. In this view, not policies but values matter most, and what voters should seek in a president is not executive effectiveness but personal virtue. Up to a point, there is much to be said for this: moral leadership *is* a crucial part of democratic politics. Ronald Reagan's optimism and charm did as much to redirect America as his tax cut and military rearmament, and contemporary conservatives will not succeed in their aim of shrinking a bloated government if the only arguments they can muster involve the gross national product and the inflation rate.

But a partial truth is not the whole truth. Politics is not religion, and values cannot be separated from policies. A president who makes speeches about the need for families to remain together while tolerating a tax structure that drives the mothers of young children into the workforce does not deserve to be called "pro-family"—not, at least, by conservatives. A president who celebrates persistence and entrepreneurship while resisting cutbacks in the government expenditures that lure poor people into dependency and that tempt corporations to substitute lobbying for research and development should not be praised by conservatives as "pro-work." And a president who calls for racial reconciliation and the recognition of individual worth while defending America's system of racial preferences should not gain a reputation for color-blindness.

Would Powell have been such a two-sided president? It is impossible to say for sure, but there is reason to think so. In a thirteen-page epilogue attached to the end of his memoir, Powell offers up a breezy analysis of contemporary politics curiously similar to that of Clinton pollster Stanley Greenberg in his new book, *Middle-Class Dreams*. Powell suggests that American voters

> are looking, in my judgment, not so much for a different party, but for a different spirit in the land, something better. How do we find our way again? How do we reestablish moral standards? How do we end the ethnic fragmentation that is making us an increasingly hyphenated people?

To these good questions, he then offers the following answer.

> We have to start thinking of America as a family. We have to stop screeching at each other, stop hurting each other, and instead start caring for, sacrificing for, and sharing with each other.

These are undigested clichés, and hence not to be taken altogether seriously. Still, they are clichés with a certain provenance. Powell's ghostwriter could, after all, have just as easily written:

> We have to start thinking of America as a team. We have to stop blaming each other, stop labelling each other, and instead start doing our best, carrying our own load, taking responsibility for ourselves.

The second pair of sentences doesn't mean much more than the first, but somehow it emits a very different message—to be brief, a conservative one.

Since the erosion of public support for liberal politics in the late 1960s, the once dynamic ideology of Harry Truman and Lyndon Johnson has survived mostly by indirection and evasion; by saying one thing on the hustings and doing another in the corridors of Congress; and by relying on a complicit press to describe liberals (of either party) as "pragmatic" or "centrist" and conservatives (of either party) as "ideological" or "extreme." The Powell quasi-candidacy raised these methods of evasion to a new level of perfection.

Ironically enough, the Powell boomlet peaked at almost exactly the same moment as the House Republicans made their bold decision to reform the Medicare program. For those conservatives who participated in the boomlet, the juxtaposition should have served as a stark reminder of the task they were sent to Washington to accomplish, and from which General Powell, by declining to run for president, has not released them.

Call This a Revolution?

In Iran or Nicaragua, a revolution occurs when a badly shaven leader harangues a street mob into frenzy, leads them through the streets to sack the palace, guns down the palace guard, writes a new constitution, and invites his supporters to pillage the country's treasury. After a couple of centuries of peace and prosperity, Americans have learned to use the word "revolution" a little more casually. To French or German ears, Newt Gingrich's promises of "revolutionary change" would sound more than a little menacing. Not in happy America, where falling computer prices spark an "information revolution," where improvement in manufacturing standards is breathlessly described as a "quality revolution," and where your local Chevy dealer celebrates the Fourth of July with "revolutionary savings."

Still, if "revolutionary change" means less in the United States than it does elsewhere, it continues to mean *something*—at the least, a substantial and permanent change of direction in public policy. One-third of the way through the Republican congressional majority's mandate, a revolution in that sense has yet to arrive.

Perhaps the word "revolution" is itself part of the problem. Another Republican "revolution" was proclaimed fifteen years ago—the Reagan revolution—and its efforts to alter the fundamental nature of Big Government were ultimately unavailing. In fact, the most successful Republican Congress of the modern era was the 80th—the one derided by Harry Truman as the "Do-Nothing Congress." What Harry Truman defined as "nothing" would now be revolution enough, far more like revolution than anything to emerge from the 104th Congress.

Certainly, the Republicans have enacted important reforms and courageously voted for large cuts in federal expenditures. The reductions in congressional staffs, the ban on proxy voting in committees, term limits for committee chairman—these reforms, resisted for decades by a Democratic leadership richly meriting Gingrich's abuse of it as "corrupt," are pumping some of the bilge water out of the ship of state.

The House's attack on federal over-regulation likewise represents real change. So does the willingness to be held to account by the electorate on the items of the Contract with America—regardless of the actual merit of those items. So, finally, do the eleven appropriations bills voted out of the House before the December 1995 shutdown of the government, which collectively contained spending cuts that averaged 4.4 percent.

But while real, the changes effected by the new Republican majority were also sharply limited. Remember, it wasn't the federal budget as a whole that was cut by 4.4 percent, but only the limited portions of it that must still go through the old appropriations procedure. Even within the discretionary portion of the budget, grotesque boondoggles that out-of-power conservatives howled against for years escaped the Republican budget-drafters unscathed. Retired Rep. Tim Penny, co-author of the abortive Penny-Kasich budget-cut plan in the 103rd Congress, ticks off some of the most egregious examples: the Legal Services Corporation and the Maritime Administration, impact aid to school districts with large numbers of federal employees, and the Appalachian Regional Commission.

And with every passing week, another increment of enthusiasm seemed to leak out of the House Republicans. Talk of abolishing the Energy, Education, Labor, and Commerce departments subsided. So did hopes for an attack on corporate subsidies: Of the $40 billion in cuts at first proposed by Budget Committee Chairman John Kasich—$15 billion worth of cuts in grants to business and the elimination of $25 billion worth of favors to specific firms and industries secreted in the tax code—only $1.5 billion emerged from the House Appropriations Committee. And don't pin all the blame on the old fossils who chair these committees: One of the most passionate defenders of the Energy Department, the Tennessee Valley Authority, the Economic Development Administration, and the Appalachian Regional Commission has been Zach Wamp, a hot-blooded freshman populist from eastern Tennessee.

The hardihood of business subsidies casts an unflattering light on the House's huge reductions in spending on regulatory activities disliked by employers: 30 percent out of the Occupational Safety and Health Administration's enforcement budget, 40 percent out of the Environmental Protection Agency's enforcement budget. A House that cuts OSHA but won't cut the Export-Import Bank lends plausibility to the jibe that the Republican Party is animated less by passion for limited government than by a subservience to the wishes of corporate America.

Indeed, on the one important vote where market principles and business interests collided, the House emphatically put business first: The Contract with America's pledge to defend property rights against regulatory takings was distorted by a last-minute amendment that defined federal water subsidies as a form of "property." The business interests that dominate the great spending committees—Agriculture, Transportation—have already learned to pay their protection money to Republicans rather than Democrats, and the well-rewarded House committee chairmen of the 104th Congress in return are transfusing cash from the taxpayers to favored industries and firms almost as enthusiastically as the committee chairmen of the 103rd.

As for the Senate—well, there the news is nearly all bad. Stephen Moore, director of fiscal policy at the Cato Institute and the editor of the House Republicans' latest manifesto, "Restoring the Dream," complains, "It's as if George Mitchell still ran the place."

Republican optimists argue that the real revolution remains "one election away"—that true reform will not come to American government until after the election of a Republican president and the strengthening of the Republican congressional majority in 1996. There's a lot to that: Big budget cuts, the redesign of vast programs like Medicare and Medicaid, the reconceiving of welfare cannot be accomplished without presidential salesmanship. But the optimistic view contains one fatal weakness: Which of the Republican presidential candidates is going to fight that fight? The most probable nominee, Robert Dole, has shown himself indifferent to— actually mystified by—serious conservatism throughout his career. The Republican revolution may indeed require one more election; unfortunately, the election required is not the one likely to occur in 1996.

And it's equally plausible—perhaps more so—that the optimists are wrong. Just as the strongly liberal Congresses elected in 1974, 1964, and 1932 did most of their damage in their first two years, so the Republican majority elected in 1994 may never be stronger than in 1995–96. Which means, that just as we are all urged to live our lives as if we could be summoned tomorrow to meet our Maker, so the Republicans would have been wise to proceed as if all they would achieve for a decade were going to be achieved by January 1997.

If anything, precedent suggests that conservative Congresses ought to proceed with even greater haste than liberal ones. Twice before in the postwar era, zealous conservative Congresses have stormed Washington, determined to redirect American government. The "Do-Nothing Congress" took the oath of office in 1947. The second was the 97th Congress, seated in 1981. Both were exhausted within two years: the Republicans who won the House in November 1946 were swept out again by Harry Truman's surprise reelection, while the Republican-conservative Democrat coalition of 1980 was shattered by the loss of northeastern GOP seats in the recession year election of 1982.

The 1947–48 Congress at least left behind a roster of enduring achievements; the Congress of 1981–82, saw its work erased as soon as it left town. The Republicans of the 104th Congress ought to have remembered the reasons for the robustness of one legislative record and the evanescence of the other.

Truman may have denounced it, but under the informal but undisputed leadership of Senator Robert Taft, the Republican House and Senate majority of 1947–48 did the following. It enacted the Taft-Hartley amendments to the Wagner Act, quashing New Deal hopes that America would become a union-dominated polity in the way that Britain, Italy, and West Germany did. It forced the repeal of wartime price controls on food and other consumer products. It put a (temporary) stop to the draft. It slashed military spending. It cut taxes. It scrapped FDR's wartime food-stamp program. It closed down Eleanor Roosevelt's experiments with federally supported day care. It limited Washington's role in the middle-class housing market to financing rather than (as liberals then wanted) construction and management too.

Perhaps most important, it rejected one after another of President Truman's projects for extending the ambit of Big Government: above all, his hopes to create an American version of Britain's new National Health Service.

Not all these victories proved permanent, of course. But even in retrospect, the twenty-year respite from activist government won by the 80th Congress amounted to more than merely a holding action. For liberals, the postwar years represented the best—perhaps the only—opportunity for the construction of a European-style social democracy in the United States. Thanks to Taft and his Republicans, that opportunity was lost.

The legacy of the Congress elected in 1980 has, sadly, proven far less durable. Not for lack of ambition: in 1981, the 97th Congress gathered the courage to vote $64 billion in domestic spending cuts, the largest round of expenditure reductions since the Eisenhower era. It merged three separate tax cuts—the Kemp-Roth reductions in marginal tax rates, the indexing of tax brackets to inflation, and a business wish list—in a gigantic reduction in government's demands upon the citizenry.

But not much of that work remains. The business tax cut was substantially retracted in 1982, Social Security payroll taxes were hiked in 1983, the tax on capital gains was hoisted up to 28 percent as part of the 1986 tax reform, and the income tax rates lowered in 1986 were pulled back up in 1990 and again in 1993. As for the spending cuts, they dissipated even faster. The U.S. spent about $5 billion on housing programs in 1983. The government spent less in 1984 than it had in 1983, less in 1985 than in 1984, less in 1986 than in 1985, less in 1987 than it had in 1986. Then, suddenly, all gains evaporated: Between 1987 and 1988, housing spending nearly sextupled, to $14 billion. By 1990, the federal government was spending more than $25 billion on housing programs. Housing is an unusually dramatic example, but in area after area of domestic discretionary spending, the restraint imposed in 1981 disappeared after 1986, and sometimes sooner.

What made the difference? The 1981–82 Congress contented itself with trimming, limiting, and containing existing programs. Between 1981 and 1988, only two federal programs were eliminated—revenue sharing with the states and the Comprehensive Employment and Training Act. The latter was promptly replaced by a new training program led through the Senate by future Vice President Quayle.

The 1947–48 Congress, though it left much of the New Deal alone, struck decisively when it moved at all. Price controls were not lifted gradually; they were abolished outright. The closed shop was not tampered with; it was prohibited. The formula for eligibility requirements for food stamps was not made more stringent; food stamps themselves were junked. Texans joke that it's useless to chop mesquite down with an ax; it will just grow back the next day. You have to blast it out of the ground with dynamite. The same holds true for federal spending programs. Leave even a smidgen of root in the soil, and within a year or two it will have regained its old size, plus some.

The Congress elected in 1994 followed the example of 1980 rather than that of 1946. Even programs that ranked at the top of its "must eliminate" list, like the National Endowment for the Arts, were not scheduled to disappear until after the 1996 election. That's a fair guarantee of their ultimate survival. Other programs will absorb budget cuts that can swiftly be reversed if political fashions change. Future Congresses will also find it easy to circumvent the Republicans' major regulatory reforms—the restrictions on unfunded mandates upon states and the stricter protection of private property rights—with technical-sounding procedural changes unlikely to excite much public indignation.

It's possible that more substantial achievements are still to come. If welfare is transformed into a block grant and handed over to the states, that would represent a policy shift as dramatic as anything that happened in the 1940s. If the Republicans redesign Medicare to bring its convulsively growing costs under control, that too would represent reform. But the portents are not especially favorable in either case. Especially not for Medicare. It is increasingly apparent that the complexities of reform—and its political risks—are flummoxing Republicans. "Restoring the Dream" strikes a distinctly nervous note whenever the topic comes up:

> Given the sheer magnitude of Medicare's financing shortfall, bipartisan cooperation is essential to establish needed, lasting reforms to keep the promise of Medicare to future generations. . . . We must begin to put Medicare on a sound financial footing, and we ought to do this on a bipartisan basis. . . .
>
> [We will] solicit broad participation from a variety of experts and the public. . . . There must be a dialogue that permits as much participation by the public as possible. By the end of the entire process, we will propose the changes necessary to preserve Medicare's solvency.

I doubt that's how Senator Taft talked when he was drafting Taft-Hartley.

Today's Republicans believe that the best guarantor of the irreversibility of their reforms is a political one: their confidence that the 1994 election signals the long-delayed arrival of the often-sighted permanent Republican majority. Because they trust that the electorate will not soon turn against them, they are not bothering to cast their new policies in ways that will be difficult to repeal. The possibility that today's cutback will regenerate under some future liberal majority seems to them far-fetched. That's quite a gamble. Even if the Republicans do hold the House of Representatives indefinitely, there's no certainty that the conservative faction within the Republican party will retain the upper hand—and no certainty that "conservatism" in the next century will go on defining itself as necessarily opposing expensive government.

In the 1996 polls, Pat Buchanan is again demonstrating what he demonstrated in 1992: the potential appeal of a free-spending, nationalistic conservatism entirely different from the conservatism of Goldwater and Reagan. Who can predict confidently that Buchanan-style conservatism will not soon carry far greater weight within the GOP?

More ominously, by betting the permanence of the 1995–96 reforms on the electorate's remaining in a conservative mood, the Republican majority is hobbling itself. If the legacy of the 104th Congress will evaporate the moment the Republicans lose power, Republicans will quickly—and not unreasonably—come to regard holding onto power as the most urgent of all their responsibilities. Unfortunately, the surest way for conservatives to hold onto power indefinitely is to delete from the definition of "conservatism" anything that might conceivably prove unpopular. A populist party will seldom long remain a principled party.

The achievements of the 104th Congress as yet appear both incomplete and disturbingly fragile. For all the excitement and commotion, the real work still lies ahead.

Righter Than Newt

The political career of Senator Phil Gramm requires that we rethink everything we believe we know about American politics. We believe we know that television demands politicians whose hair is shiny, whose voices are mellifluous, and who exude cheerful humility. We believe we know that Americans abhor extremes and mistrust ideology. We believe we know that government programs are incradicable and that costly middle-class entitlements are hugely popular. We believe we know all these things. Gramm believes we're wrong.

Gramm's hair does not shine, and his Georgia accent is as thick as gumbo. He is neither cheerful nor humble. He makes fewer political compromises than almost anyone else in public life. He wants to abolish affirmative action, write a balanced-budget amendment to the federal Constitution, slash taxes, and eliminate roughly a third of the domestic budget, with the biggest cuts coming from programs intended for low-income people. And he is utterly convinced that what he wants, America wants. In sum, Gramm is inviting Republicans to wager the 1996 presidential election on a breathtaking gamble: that the voters are at last ready to repudiate liberalism completely.

Should Phil Gramm somehow win the 1996 Republican nomination (and assuming that Bill Clinton retains the Democratic nomination), then the 1996 election will present the voters with a choice between two men starkly different and yet strangely similar—two equal and opposite halves of their generation's experience. Gramm and Clinton are only four years apart in age. Both come from poor southern families, and both owe their success in life to the great postwar expansion of higher education. Both have spent virtually their entire working lives in the public sector, and both are married to high-achieving professional women. Neither has served in the armed forces—which would make 1996 the first race between two nonveterans since 1944. For both men, modern government was an accomplished fact by the time they entered politics: they are inheritors of the Great Society. But whereas Clinton accepts this inheritance with hardly any reservations, Gramm has rebelled against it. There is thus perhaps one more thing we shall have to revise if Gramm wins his prize, and that is our conventional understanding of who the young people of the 1960s really were and what they really believed, at the time and in the years since.

President Clinton may have imbibed the free and easy ways of that decade; Gramm remains as driven and self-controlled as any upwardly mobile poor boy in a Victorian novel. Asked to assess the quality of the Clinton White House staff, Gramm sniffs, "They have a sloppy look about them." Sloppy Gramm is not, and he does not tolerate sloppiness in those around him. His shirts are always meticulously pressed, and the down-home remarks he makes in public have all been carefully weighed in advance. Unlike the president, Gramm is scrupulously punctual. In the course of his ascent President Clinton somehow absorbed some of the relaxed manners of his aristocratic heroes, the Roosevelts and the Kennedys. It's understandable that—as Clinton's pollsters discovered to their horror in 1992—many Americans assumed he was born in comfort. But nobody could ever mistake Gramm for anything but a self-made man.

Perhaps it is Gramm's thrusting qualities that most strongly mark the difference between his conservatism and that of his antecedents on the Republican right—Ronald Reagan, Barry Goldwater, and Robert Taft. Unlike Taft's, Gramm's speech is demotic. Only recently has Gramm's accent begun to thin; he still often forgets his staff's advice to refer to his "mother," not his "mamma." Unlike Goldwater, Gramm calculates political risks carefully. Shortly before the November 8, 1994 congressional election Gramm made a campaign appearance in behalf of a young Republican congressional challenger in Arizona. He listened to the young man deliver a bombastic, foolish speech and afterward took him aside for some unsweetened advice. "There are only two issues when running against an incumbent," he said. "Her record, and I'm not a kook. Forget the feel-good stuff. Say, This is her record; this is what I'm for. If a subject can't elect you to Congress, don't talk about it."

And unlike Reagan, Gramm does his homework. Reagan was a man of feeling; Gramm is a man of intellect. His mind burns at a higher wattage than that of any other senator save Daniel Patrick Moynihan. Reagan never really understood the institutions he had pledged to reform; Gramm has mastered the details of American government better than any other national Republican figure. Again unlike Reagan, Gramm is his own handler. By the time Reagan ran for president in 1980, he had been a star for more than forty-five years. He expected people to take care of him. Gramm does not. He carries his own garment bag and does his own thinking. That cruel joke about Reagan—"It's not that Reagan lacks principles; it's that he doesn't understand the ones he has"—does not apply to Gramm. He has thought his principles through, he recognizes that they will exact substantial human costs, and he has decided that those costs are outweighed by the potential benefits.

It is this ideological rigor, unsoftened by any of Reagan's telegenic benignity, that best accounts for Gramm's reputation for "meanness," an accusation that has been hurled not only by squishy liberals but also by conservatives. Michael Barone, the increasingly right-tilting co-author of the *Almanac of American Politics,* has written of Gramm. "There is a note of anger to him—a sharp edge of hostility toward those whose view of America is quite different. In this friendly country, angry candidates—Pat Buchanan, Jerry Brown are 1992's examples—do not wear well." In her book *Life, Liberty and the Pursuit of Happiness,* Peggy Noonan quotes an acquaintance's put-down: " '[Gramm's] best friends don't like him.' "

In fact, though, Gramm in person is anything but angry or harsh. He may lack the anemic quality we call niceness, but he's a witty and polite man. His friends do seem to like him: he and Senator John McCain, of Arizona—the gallant ex-POW—spent the two weeks before the 1994 election hopping about the Southwest together in a tiny aircraft, shared a case of flu, and by day eight were still swapping jokes with warmth and kindliness. Gramm's marriage has lasted twenty-five years and is, insofar as outsiders can or ought to judge, a close one; his two college-age sons seem to be well-adjusted young men. Turnover on his staff is low; Gramm is not one of those senators who shriek at their employees or ask them to perform demeaning tasks.

On the other hand, those who know the Senate point out that Gramm is not popular with his colleagues there, not even the

Republicans among them. He takes few pains to disguise his pride in his ability or his awareness of his colleagues' limitations. He does not twinkle with good humor, as Reagan did. Nor does he bother to disguise his fierce pursuit of the presidency. Presidential candidates used to feign reluctance. When Franklin Delano Roosevelt flew to the 1932 Democratic Convention in Chicago to accept his party's nomination in person, many were startled. Until then nominees had been expected to wait at home for a delegation to arrive on their doorstep and plead with them to heed their country's call. Even today we retain vague feelings that the job should seek the man. But for more than a year beforehand, Gramm told anyone who asked that he intended to run for President in 1996. His directness can shock more circumspect souls. Shortly after the 1994 election, a prominent Republican who has been raising money for Jack Kemp for nearly a decade paid a call on Gramm in the company of one of Kemp's top aides to congratulate Gramm on his success as chairman of the party's senatorial campaign. After half a minute or so of pleasantries, Gramm fixed his eyes on his visitor and, looking past the Kemp aide's reddening face, bluntly got down to business: "You know and I know that Jack's nowhere in this race. There are only three candidates worth mentioning: Lamar Alexander, Bob Dole, and me. You've got to back me."

Still, ambitious politicians are not unknown in American life. The presidency didn't fall into Bill Clinton's lap either. And if Gramm lacks Reagan's ability to project good cheer through a television camera, so does Bob Dole. Neither ambition nor the whims of the mass media sufficiently explain Gramm's unflattering public image. No, if Gramm is thought to be uniquely mean, that is owing to something more substantial: his uniquely uncompromising politics.

Liberalism today plays much the same role in social life that Christianity played in late Victorian Britain; increasing numbers of people have come to suspect that it is not valid, even as they find themselves utterly unable to imagine any alternative source of truth. With the Sea of Faith withdrawn, Matthew Arnold groaned, this world *"Hath really neither joy, nor love, nor light,/ Nor certitude, nor peace, nor help for pain. . . ."* But Gramm refuses to cross himself at the liberal chapel. Many conservatives who attended college in the 1960s were swept up enough in those guilt-tortured years to have acquired the need to prove to their liberal friends that they are decent folks despite their repellent ideology: "I'm for cutting spending—*except for antipoverty programs.*" "I'm conservative—*but I consider myself a feminist.*" "I object to quotas—*but I want vigorous enforcement of the rest of the civil-rights laws.*" "I think you're mistaken—*but I respect your good intentions.*"

Gramm concedes nothing. "I've never had a campaign that I didn't have an opponent who was rich, and who had rich parents, telling me about poor people," he says. "I'm not going to be cowed by people who want to accuse me of being anti-poor. I'm not going to be swayed by people who say, 'You have no compassion.' I have great compassion. I think of the unwed mother who is working as a cook in a little restaurant, working ten or eleven hours a day. She is barely making ends meet. It is wrong that people who aren't working are getting more money than she is. I think she ought to get to keep more of what she earns. I don't think it's fair that because she is working, she gets no medical coverage, or has difficulty getting it, and somebody who doesn't work gets the best in the world."

In Gramm's mind, what that woman needs is for government simply to leave her alone. "My view on life is very much colored by who I am, and where I grew up, and how my people succeeded. And by my wife's story. My wife's grandfather came to this country as an indentured laborer to work in the sugarcane fields. Her father was the first Asian-American ever to be an officer of a sugar company. She became chairman of the CFTC [Commodity Futures Trading Commission] under Reagan and Bush, and regulated sugarcane futures. That's America in action. Anybody who's gonna try to tell me America doesn't work—they're wasting their breath. It can't be done, I can't be convinced."

His political philosophy might be summed up as Reaganism in three dimensions, the third being depth. He does not buy the happy message of the supply-siders of the early 1980s: low enough tax rates will pump out enough revenues to obviate any big change in social programs. To be sure, Gramm wants to cut taxes. On the stump he complains, "In 1950 the average American family with two children sent one dollar out of every fifty dollars it earned to Washington, D.C. And they probably thought it was too much. Today that family is sending one dollar in every four dollars to Washington. In twenty years, if there are no new programs, . . . the figure will be one dollar out of every three dollars."

However, he scorns those who "want the benefits of limited

government but not the costs." Gramm envisions a radical recon-
ception of the functions of the federal government. He would
cheerfully spend more money on defense. "If the lion and the lamb
are about to lie down together in the world," he says, "it's very
important that the United States of America be the lion" (a motto
so pleasing to him that he has had it framed and hung on his office
wall). He would build necessary physical infrastructure—although
"whether every airport in America needs to be a remake of the Taj
Mahal or not is an open question." Beyond that, he says, he would
put the federal government on a budget. And the main targets of
his budgeting would be means-tested programs: Medicaid, Supplemental Security Income, food stamps, low-income energy assistance, and Aid to Families with Dependent Children. As Gramm
incessantly puts it, "I'm going to ask those riding in the wagon to
get out and help the rest of us pull it."

Now, Gramm is intimately familiar with the federal budget. He
knows perfectly well that the bulk of federal spending is lavished
on middle- and upper-income taxpayers. He claims that when Secretary of Labor Robert Reich attacked federal business subsidies in
a November 1994 speech, he offered to sponsor a bill eliminating
them. And his plan to reform public and private health insurance
would have the effect of hitting Medicare's middle-class beneficiaries with a quadrupling or quintupling of the present deductible of
$600-plus. The idea is complicated, but essentially, health insur-
ance and Medicare for routine expenses would be eliminated.
Instead employers would contribute to special tax-advantaged savings accounts—usually known as "medical IRAs." The difference
between deposits into those accounts and money actually spent on
health care each year would be the saver's to roll over or pay taxes
on and keep. Insurance—whether private or Medicare—would not
start to pick up health costs until after the first $2,500 or $3,000 a
year. Since about 80 percent of Americans spend less than $3,000
a year on health care, medical IRAs would reorient American medicine away from insurance to direct payment by patients. The
advantages of patient payment are potentially vast—almost as vast
as the likely shock to a middle class that by and large feels content
with the health care that it gets.

Likewise, Gramm's promise that people who have contributed
to the Social Security system will get their money back—and his
omission of any promise of more—clearly implies that Social Security will play a much smaller role for future retirees than it plays

now. Still, Gramm is no neo-liberal. For all their faults, he regards Social Security and Medicare as "earned benefits," which deserve gentler treatment than means-tested welfare programs. Most of those he'd like to scrap, and use the money saved to double the per-child tax exemption to $5,000 from the present $2,450.

When challenged to justify the apparent unfairness of this discrepancy, he bristles. One set of benefits was paid for, the other wasn't. Isn't that reason enough for the difference? He angrily rejects any imputation of unfairness. "I'm trying to help people who are on welfare. I'm not hurting them. The government hurt them. The government took away from them something more important than this money. They took away their initiative, they took away a substantial measure of their freedom, they took away in many cases their morality. They corroded their morality, their drive, their pride. I want to help them get that back. . . . I want to do it because I love them, because I want them to be Americans. And their children and grandchildren will thank us."

A President Gramm would attempt to enact a comprehensive and radical free-market program, more radical than that of Newt Gingrich's House Republicans. With the stroke of a pen he would repeal the executive orders that enforce affirmative action. Environmental and other rules would be subject to a new regulation requiring Washington to compensate property owners if any federal rule reduced the value of their holdings by more than 25 percent. But the issues on which Gramm's attention is fixed are the cost of government to the ordinary worker and the dangerous allurement of welfare. "Ordinary people" figure large in his speeches. "America is not a great and powerful country because the most brilliant and talented people in the world came to live here. It's ordinary people—people who would have been peasants anywhere else—who were able to do extraordinary things." That is, Gramm insists, his own story—but if there's one thing that Phil Gramm isn't, it's an ordinary person.

The future senator was born in Fort Benning, Georgia, in 1942. His mother's family name was Scroggins: Gramm knows little more about her family than that they were Scotch-Irish and that his grandmother's father and grandfather fought for the Confederacy at Shiloh. Gramm's mother had been divorced young, and she had been obliged to work for a time in a cotton mill to support her two sons by that first marriage. Her second husband, Kenneth Gramm, the senator's father, was the son of an immigrant from

Germany. He joined the U.S. Army at age fifteen, served along the Mexican border during the First World War, and rose to the rank of sergeant. For many years he taught at the infantry school at Fort Benning, outside Columbus. Just before he was to have been shipped out to Europe, after D-Day, he suffered an incapacitating heart attack and stroke. He lived for the next thirteen years as an invalid. Mrs. Gramm got herself trained as a practical nurse, and earned a living caring for well-to-do patients in their homes. That could have been an embittering experience. It wasn't. His mother "would come home and tell us that basically the difference between them and us is that they worked harder," Gramm says. "We could be like them. My mother would drive by the nicest house in Columbus, Georgia, and she would say, 'You could have a house like that if you worked hard for it.'"

At first the young Gramm was not persuaded. He was an indifferent student. He relishes telling the story of how he failed the third, seventh, and ninth grades. He diffidently suggests that he may have been dyslexic, or that he may have resented his disabled father's too-determined efforts to push him along. Whatever the explanation, his ambition ignited soon after his father's death, and he graduated from high school with honors in 1961. He was only the second person in his entire clan ever to have completed high school; his half-brother Don White had been the first.

The Army had given the Gramms some insurance money, but it proved insufficient to pay for both boys' college educations. Gramm's half-brother joined the Army: Gramm himself moved to Atlanta, held part-time jobs, studied by correspondence, married his first wife at age nineteen, and took a bachelor's degree in three years at the University of Georgia and a Ph.D. in economics in a little less than three years more. He was appointed to the faculty of Texas A&M, the University of Texas's less prestigious rival, in the fall of 1967. He had made it into the middle class.

That was a time of upheaval in America, but the turmoil did not touch Professor Gramm. He was entranced by economics— "These were powerful ideas that explained the world that I knew"—and saw that he did not know nearly enough about his discipline. "The University of Georgia did not have a very good graduate program. Everybody I was competing with knew more math, more stat, than I did. So I audited all of our Ph.D. programs, and in essence got two Ph.D.s." To this day Gramm despairs over gaps in his knowledge. "The easiest way for me to get melancholy is to walk over to the Library of Congress and look down those endless stacks of books, and realize there's information in there I need to know and am going to die not knowing."

He claims to have stayed aloof from politics in those early years, except for voting for Goldwater in 1964. As he tells it, the racial agonies of the desegregating South left scarcely a mark on him. Asked about it now, he begins by asserting that segregation was "obviously wrong." But although he attended segregated schools throughout his childhood, and although the University of Georgia "was integrated the year before I came or the year after I came" (it was the year before: January of 1961), the civil-rights struggle seems not to have galvanized him.

Neither did Vietnam. His half-brother fought in Vietnam, and so did many of Gramm's students at Texas A&M; for much of that time he himself, as a graduate student and as a married man, was exempt from service. His support for America's aims in Vietnam never wavered. "To me, Vietnam was about what Korea was about: it was about containing communism." He had only one concern about the war: "that we were losing it."

After his first marriage ended, he filled his time coaching Boys Club football, and bought a few rental properties to supplement his income. He worshiped three times a week as an Episcopal acolyte. Those were his 1960s. *The Big Chill* notwithstanding, they were also the sixties of millions or tens of millions of other striving, ambitious young people.

Gramm remarried in 1970. Like Hillary Rodham Clinton, the second Mrs. Gramm came from a social position loftier than her husband's. Wendy Lee attended Wellesley and went on to complete a Ph.D. in economics at Northwestern University. It wasn't Miss Lee's eyes or ankles that initially stirred Gramm's interest in her: it was her dissertation. He liked it so much that he invited himself to New York to sit in on her interview for a job at Texas A&M. Afterward he walked her to the door, helped her on with her coat, and said, "As a senior member of the faculty, I would be especially interested in you coming to Texas A&M." This overture, he ruefully reminisces in a much-told anecdote, was not immediately successful. "She looks at me and [I can see her think] 'Yuck.' So I went back in and said to the people at the interview table, 'We're going to convince her to come to Texas A&M, and I'm going to marry her.' So anyway, she did, and I did."

As Wendy Lee Gramm's background parallels Hillary Rodham

Clinton's, so would her role in her husband's Administration. Mrs. Gramm tells friends that she would downplay politics, that she would set her sights on becoming "the nation's first Rollerblading First Lady." They don't believe her. She is a woman of formidable intelligence (she's probably a better technical economist than her husband) and strong free-market views. Republican marriages formed in the 1940s, 1950s, and early 1960s are often riven by a silent ideological divide: in the tumult of the sixties the wife went left and the husband didn't. This familiar feature of Washington social life is now coming to its natural end as the tumult retreats further and further into the past. Unlike George Bush and Ronald Reagan, Phil Gramm at home hears advice that comes from the ideological right.

Academia did not content the Gramms for long. Spurred by his dislike of inflation and rising taxes, Phil Gramm decided to run for office. For some time he had been soliciting speaking engagements at eastern Texas chambers of commerce and publishing articles. It was an op-ed piece in the *Wall Street Journal* that brought him national attention. The piece pointed out that the world had seemed in the mid-nineteenth century to be exhausting its supplies of its main lighting fuel, whale oil. Prices rose and rose . . . until some venturesome profit-seeker tried burning petroleum instead. Emboldened by the applause of his chamber-of-commerce audiences, Gramm decided to challenge then-Senator Lloyd Bentsen in the Texas Democratic primary in 1976. It was a breathtaking act of bravado. Bentsen was a rich man, an effective senator, and a skilled campaigner who had dispatched George Bush in 1970. Even as a publicity stunt, running against Bentsen was risky. But the race was no stunt: at the beginning Gramm truly believed he would win. "I'd never lost at anything in my life," he says. He was crushed; he received only 28 percent of the vote. He was also broke. He had put $50,000—all the money the Gramms possessed—into the campaign, and every dime of it had been spent. He decided to try again anyway, and in 1978 entered the House of Representatives as a Democrat for a district that stretched from the northern reaches of Houston to the southern suburbs of Fort Worth, and that encompassed the seat of Texas A&M, in College Station.

Almost immediately, Gramm embroiled himself in conflict with the head of the Texas Democratic delegation, Jim Wright, then the House Majority Leader. "Jim Wright could never understand me.

He kept wondering what it was I wanted. He kept asking my Democratic colleagues from Texas, who'd come to Congress the same year I did, what was it I wanted," In Gramm's account, Wright held out the apple of temptation, explaining how conservative Democrats could be excused from certain votes if the leadership didn't need them and how they could remain free to criticize the party at home, and offering him choice committee assignments. Finally, after the Democrats' 1980 debacle, Gramm extracted from Wright the assignment he had coveted from the beginning: the Budget Committee.

Wright, who resigned in disgrace from the speakership in 1989, remembers things a little differently. In a written statement he recalls that Gramm "came to me pleading for my help [to get onto the Budget Committee]. I explained . . . that these . . . were choice plums reserved for colleagues on whom the Democratic caucus could count when the chips were down. [Gramm] promised to be [a] team player. . . . A relic of the old Texas school which values a handshake over a gilt-edged bond, I took [him] at his word."

Whether he forced or begged his way onto the Budget Committee, Gramm quickly dominated it. In his memoirs the former Reagan budget director David Stockman identifies Gramm as one of only three representatives—Jim Jones of Oklahoma, then the chairman of the Budget Committee, and Leon Panetta, then a Democratic member of the committee, being the other two—who thoroughly understood the budget. Stockman, not an indulgent judge of others' weaknesses, unhesitatingly describes Gramm as "brilliant"; Gramm became his partner and floor leader in the House.

Gramm willingly left the pleasures of tax cutting to others and instead assumed the unpopular chore of producing matching cuts in domestic expenditures. This was another of Gramm's gambles, one certain to win him the undying enmity of the Democratic leadership. He plunged ahead regardless. With Delbert L. Latta of Ohio as Republican co-sponsor in the House, Gramm and Stockman outmaneuvered the leadership of the Democratic Party, and won the day for the Administration-backed Gramm-Latta budget in May 1981.

Those were fevered days for conservatives, dramatic days. As the crucial vote in the House Representatives neared, Gramm's bloc of conservative southern Democrats, the "Boll Weevils," came under intense pressure from the Democratic leadership to stay with the party. Jim Jones had designed a less draconian budget plan of his own, and many of the Boll Weevils felt tempted to heed their party leadership. In his memoirs David Stockman tells what happened next. At a meeting in the office of the most important of the Boll Weevils, Mississippi's Sonny Montgomery, "the group's chairman, Charlie Stenholm of Texas, asked the members for their opinion of [the Jim Jones alternative]."

> One by one they said it was a *reasonable compromise* and that it would allow them to work with the Democratic leadership while at the same time promoting President Reagan's goals.
>
> Gramm waited until everyone had said his piece. . . . It was clear to him, Gramm said, that if William Barrett Travis, commander of the American forces at the Alamo, had asked for a debate instead of drawing the famous line in the sand, then "there never would have been a battle."
>
> This was followed by five minutes of shouting. Jack Hightower of Texas pointedly reminded Gramm that everyone who crossed the line at the Alamo died. There was a murmur of assent at this.
>
> "Yes," said Gramm, "but the ones who didn't cross the line died, too. Only no one remembers their names."

Gramm-Latta carried the day. Then, after the Senate also passed an Administration-approved budget, Gramm and Stockman crafted Gramm-Latta II, a package of spending cuts that "reconciled" the difference between revenues and spending in the budget, and dashed what remained of the Democratic leadership's hopes of rendering the Reagan Administration's program stillborn.

At first it seemed that Gramm had bought his success in 1981 at the expense of his political career. The Republicans lost twenty-six seats in the 1982 midterm elections, and House Speaker Tip O'Neill and Jim Wright seized the opportunity to take revenge on the Democratic defectors. Gramm was stripped of his Budget Committee seat. He promptly resigned from the Democratic Party and reaffiliated as a Republican. Then, although he was not obliged to, he resigned his seat and asked for a special election. It was a desperate fight, but Gramm's stock quip to his campaign audiences, "I had to choose between Tip O'Neill and y'all, and I decided to stand with y'all," achieved the desired effect: he won his seat back. The following year he ran for the Senate seat left open by the resignation of John Tower, Texas's first post-Reconstruction Republican senator, and won again.

In his first year as a senator, a time when tradition calls for deference to the senior members of the institution, Gramm rolled the dice again, and produced the Gramm-Rudman-Hollings deficit-reduction amendment. In what Gramm's co-producer Warren Rudman, of New Hampshire, described as "a bad idea whose time has come," the law set a series of deficit targets and instituted mechanisms for automatic across-the-board reductions in both domestic and defense spending if those targets were not met. For conservatives, who had lost control of the House in 1982 and whose grip on the Senate was tenuous at best in 1985, Gramm-Rudman represented an appalling risk. It conceded the principle that the defense budget should be constrained by budgetary limits rather than by the Pentagon's estimation of Soviet capabilities. Worse still, it took no position at all as to whether the deficit targets would be met by raising taxes or by reducing spending. Gramm cheerfully bet the house anyway, and defends his bet to this day.

"The beauty of the Gramm-Rudman idea was that it put the fat in the fire," he says. "We could then put out the fire either by raising taxes or by cutting spending. So different people could see it producing different results. And since we had nothing like a majority on this issue, it was necessary that it be viewed as a tool, so that people would think they could do various things with the tool. I thought I could do something."

And to a degree it worked. Over the next five years, spending growth did slow and the deficit did shrink. True, Gramm-Rudman's deficit targets were often met only by chicanery—by anticipating revenues and moving expenses off-budget—but in fiscal year 1989 the deficit had slipped to three percent of gross domestic product and the federal government's share of the economy had inched down to 22.1 percent, roughly where it had stood in 1980.

The later 1980s turned out to be fallow years for Gramm. After the loss of the Senate by the Republicans in 1986, Gramm could no longer enact legislation. His greatest accomplishment in those days was a negative one: he foresaw the danger in partly deregulating the savings-and-loans industry. In 1982 Gramm had voted against the act that freed savings-and-loans to enter non-housing lines of business. He says, "I was always worried about this sleepy little regulator of housing lending [the Home Loan Bank Board, which oversaw thrifts] ... suddenly regulating people who were residual earners in the fried-chicken business." As the financial condition of the S&Ls deteriorated and regulators closed in, Gramm introduced legislation to tax S&Ls to beef up the deposit-insurance fund. This prescience alienated him from the rest of the Texas delegation, because Texas was home to more troubled thrifts than any other state. And it tossed him into renewed combat with Jim Wright, the thrifts' main defender in Congress—a fact that may even have helped inspire Gramm's suspicion of the faltering industry.

The pace of events quickened again for Gramm after 1989. But this time the course he took nearly proved disastrous, at least for his reputation with his conservative base: he involved himself in the negotiations that led to President Bush's ill-fated 1990 budget deals. The details are serpentine, but in their wake Gramm-Rudman had vanished, and the top rate of income tax had hopped to 31 percent from Ronald Reagan's 28 percent. Gramm now defends his actions in 1990 on grounds of party loyalty and personal affection for George Bush. But two other considerations must have entered his mind as well. At the time George Bush seemed certain to be re-elected to the presidency in 1992. Bush's support, or at least his benign neutrality, would thus be indispensable to anyone planning a run for the presidency in 1996—especially if that anyone hailed from Bush's home state, and doubly especially considering that there was a sitting vice president who would have to be knocked aside. Alternatively, if Bush's backing could not be won, Gramm would need an iron grip on the loyalties of Texas—and its big donors—in the run-up to the 1996 cycle. In order to clamp that grip on the state, Gramm retreated from his accustomed ultrapure anti-pork-barrel stance. He helped pull the huge supercollider project to Texas and championed the Houston-based manned space station, while also showing new zeal for Texas's agriculture interests, among them the much-ridiculed mohair subsidy. Those prizes also required presidential good will—which helped to pull him into Bush's budgetary thickets. And unlike Newt Gingrich, who broke ranks with Bush, Gramm, once stuck, could not easily walk away. In the end Gramm cast his vote against the final budget deal, but quietly.

Washington conservatives may have felt irritated at Gramm in 1990; back home he was more popular than ever. He won re-election that year with 60.2 percent of the vote, a larger margin than any Texas senatorial candidate had garnered since 1958. He demonstrated stunning fund-raising powers, too. A single 1990 event, staged in the Houston Astrodome, raked in well over $2 million. "You can't be more powerful in Washington than you are at home" is a Gramm maxim. Awed, his Senate colleagues named him chairman of the Republicans' overall senatorial fund-raising drive for the 1992 and 1994 election cycles.

Then, as movie serials used to intone, fate stepped in. To the astonishment of everyone—not least fainthearted Democratic hopefuls like Mario Cuomo and Bill Bradley—the Bush Administration disintegrated and the Republicans found themselves out of power. Dan Quayle was suddenly struck from the Republican line of succession, and a new job needed to be filled: leader of the opposition. Gramm grabbed it.

While Dole and even Gingrich took months to decide that they would not negotiate with Clinton on a health-care plan, and while Jack Kemp, Dick Cheney, and Lamar Alexander vanished onto the speaking circuit, Gramm immediately threw himself into implacable confrontation. "I think Hillary Clinton and I were the only two people who read the whole fill. She loved it and I hated it," he later said. He assembled a panel of senators and representatives to travel the country campaigning against the plan. As conservative criticism punctured the plan and public support leaked away, other Republicans rushed to take up the position that Gramm had occupied months before. But he had been there first, when the spot had looked dangerous, and he did not let anyone forget it.

Probably nowhere else in America but Texas—and certainly in no other large state—could a man with such radical views on economics, and such relatively bland views on social issues, rise so high so fast. Nor is Gramm alone. Two of the three most senior Republicans in the House—the Majority Leader, Dick Armey; and the majority whip, Tom DeLay—are also Texans who combine economic radicalism with understated positions on the hot-button issues that excite the Republican faithful elsewhere in the South. A fourth Texan, Bill Archer, chairs the Ways and Means Committee.

Historically, the Republican Party has taken its tone from one particular state or region at a time: Henry Cabot Lodge's Massachusetts, Robert Taft's Ohio, Ronald Reagan's southern California. Today Gramm's Texas supplies the party with its strongest themes and ideas. Except for Florida, Texas is the most urbanized state in the South: more than 80 percent of the population lives in cities. (In Newt Gingrich's Georgia the figure is a little above 60 percent.) And the Texas Republican Party, since its emergence in the

1970s as a serious political force, has been a metropolitan party, drawing its explosively growing strength—it elected three times as many officeholders in 1994 as in 1982—first from Dallas and environs, a little later from Houston, and only very recently from the rest of the state.

The people who live in and around Texas's cities earn their livings in increasingly sophisticated ways. Although far from wealthy (household income ranks thirty-second in the nation), Texans have managed to diversify their economy beyond oil and agriculture. High-technology companies around Austin and Dallas, and shipping and financial-services companies near Houston and Dallas, employ a rapidly growing population of college graduates, many of them newcomers to the state. Of Texas's 17 million people, 4.3 million were born in the other forty-nine states, and another 1.7 million were born abroad.

In some southern states—Virginia is the clearest example— newcomers have leaned to the left of the rest of the population. That hasn't happened in Texas. On the contrary: Louis Dubose, the editor of the liberal *Texas Observer* newspaper, argues that the heart of fundamentalist Christianity in Texas is not the countryside but the megachurches that line the interstate connecting Dallas and Fort Worth and the beltways around other big cities. The Christian conservatives at the Texas state Republican convention last year, Dubose jokes, weren't wearing farmers' "gimme" caps; they were wearing the plastic pocket-protectors beloved of engineers and computer designers. Just as Islamic fundamentalism wins converts not in the villages but among the uprooted and semi-modernized people of the cities of Algeria and Egypt, so Christian fundamentalism in Texas seems to have won some of its following among the first-generation college graduates who have left small towns in eastern Texas or the Midwest to work for Hewlett-Packard or Electronic Data Systems in Dallas County.

Their religious beliefs do not, however, blind high-tech Christians to the fact that they draw their livelihoods from an integrated world economy. Conservatives throughout the South flirt dangerously with protectionism, Newt Gingrich not least Gramm never has. He will, though, take trouble to accommodate his constituents' social views. Although wary of school prayer ("It's got to be very strictly limited, and it's got to be voluntary. You can't empower zealots"), he opposes abortion, and in his 1984 campaign for the Senate he made gleeful use of the fact that his opponent, Lloyd

Doggett, had received money from a fund-raising event at a gay strip club. Last year he declined to condemn California's Proposition 187, which denies schooling and other benefits to illegal aliens. He artfully weaves religious imagery into his speeches.

Gramm hopes to persuade Republican primary voters, especially Christian conservatives, that his economic conservatism is cultural conservatism. "If you are talking about values issues," he says, "what is more value-laden than the welfare system? What is more value-related than the tax cuts? Aren't we talking about values when we're talking about stopping the subsidizing of conceiving illegitimate children? Aren't we talking about values when we're talking about cutting spending and doubling the dependent exemption for children?"

Values talk inevitably raises the question of Gramm's own morality. His political conduct has been called into question at least twice. In 1989 the Federal Elections Commission fined his campaign $30,000 for violations relating to his 1984 Senate race. Then there was what some see as a $50,000 personal gift from a Texas homebuilder and savings-and-loan operator, Jerry Stiles. At Gramm's request, Stiles, a longtime supporter, flew a crew of carpenters to Maryland to finish a summer house Gramm owns on the Eastern Shore. Gramm paid Stiles for the work, but an investigation later found that Stiles had charged Gramm $50,000 less than the cost of the job. Then, when Stiles's S&L ran into trouble, he asked Gramm for help. There is no evidence that Gramm interceded improperly for Stiles or that Gramm even knew of Stiles's $50,000 loss. When the loss finally came to light, Gramm wrote Stiles a check for $50,000 and laid the matter before the Senate Ethics Committee. The committee ruled that Gramm had owed Stiles nothing, and Stiles refunded Gramm's money. Stiles seems to have hoped to curry favor with Gramm; five years later, however, no evidence has appeared that the currying worked or that Gramm received anything like an illegal gratuity.

Still, it's a strange story, given that this hyperideological politician rests much of his case to his fellow Republicans on his organizational acumen. Gramm contends that a run for the presidency will cost more than $44 million in 1996. "That's a lot of money to raise when somebody can give you only a thousand dollars. I think management and organization are things that are greatly undervalued in politics. The question is, who can put together this forty-four-million-dollar corporate entity? Who can set up a structure to manage it? No one running for office has ever had to do what you're going to have to do in this election to win the nomination, and that is you're going to have to raise all this money early, you're going to have to run in fifteen or twenty states at the same time, without being the party nominee, without having every political operative in the party working for you—which they will after you get the nomination."

Of all the similarities between Gramm and Clinton, the one perhaps that matters most is their agreement that one of the most important issues facing the nation is the apparent dwindling of the prospects of the middle-class American family. Both of them keenly remember a time, not so very long ago, when opportunities seemed to abound. Today's world seems somehow tighter, less expansive. Clinton's explanation of what has gone wrong is technical: changes in the world economy, new technologies and ways of work that have raised the value of trained labor relative to unskilled and semi-skilled. Gramm's analysis is ideological: "We've gotten off track. It's like a football team. We stopped winning because we stopped doing the things that made us winners. We started to reward people who were doing things that did not represent productive behavior. We started to penalize people who did." It's not some global economic climacteric that is ailing America, in Gramm's eyes: American living standards are eroding because of decisions made in America—because the productive are overtaxed and the unproductive are overprotected.

Fiercely and uncompromisingly, Gramm intends to reverse that distribution of rewards and penalties. Nervous Republicans may hear in his fierceness an ominous warning of a debacle to come—another 1964. But the country's mood has shifted dramatically since those days. Republicans seeking national office need no longer hew to the center.

Which is why Gramm's prediction that he would emerge as the main rival to Bob Dole seemed credible. Who else, after all, was there? Former Vice President Dan Quayle could appeal to Republican sentiment that he was treated unfairly by the detested liberal media and to the growing national consensus that his controversial "Murphy Brown" remarks have proved right after all. But he would have had to campaign bearing the stigma of defeat and without an institutional base. Richard Nixon pulled off the trick in 1968, but—to adapt the joke that will haunt Quayle for the rest of his career—Dan Quayle is no Richard Nixon. Republicans don't like to admit it, but they know that the reason the media image of Quayle as a lightweight has endured is that he *is* a lightweight.

Ex officio, Pete Wilson ought to have ranked high on any list of potential nominees. Not only could he tap the fantastic wealth of California, but he artfully crafted a new ideological position that might be crudely summed up as Go, left on sex (he's pro-choice and sympathetic to gay rights), right on race (immigration and affirmative action), and up the middle on economics. And yet Wilson suffered two daunting political handicaps: as governor, he raised taxes to balance his budget—a sin he has since tried to expiate by calling for a 15-percent tax cut—and in the 1994 campaign he repeatedly promised to serve out his term.

Among the other prominent governors, William Weld, of Massachusetts, saw his hopes run aground on the rocks of the recession of the early 1990s. To lift the veto that the party's social conservatives would put on him for his support for abortion and gay rights, he would have needed a breathtaking record of tax and spending cuts. He didn't have it. Tommy Thompson of Wisconsin, Christine Whitman of New Jersey, and John Engler of Michigan, dropped no hints that they even considered a run.

The year 1996 ought to have been Jack Kemp's year. Kemp was the only other Republican to have offered a program as coherent, as principled, and as intensely felt as Gramm's. Had he resigned from President Bush's Cabinet over the abandonment of the "no new taxes" pledge, he would have sealed his claim on the 1996 nomination. Instead he is exiting into history as a man who never quite seized his moment.

The collapse of Kemp's candidacy left Gramm virtually alone on the free-market Republican right. That should have attracted other credible conservatives into the race, including the most powerful of them all, House Speaker Newt Gingrich. But it wasn't going to be easy for Gingrich to plunge in. His congressional work was too pressing. If he had sacrificed the Republican agenda in order to campaign, he would have opened himself to damaging accusations within the party. A Gingrich presidential campaign could also spark uncomfortable demands that he release the names of the contributors to his political-action committee, GOPAC. Besides, Gingrich had just won the job he spent twenty years working for. He would have to be a very discontented personality indeed to jeopardize it by immediately reaching for another one.

The basis of Robert Dole's claim was, essentially, seniority. He ran for vice prresident in 1976, finished second in the 1988 primaries, and serves now as the Senate Majority Leader. He is hugely respected inside the party. Even conservatives who resented his antipathy to supply-side economics in the 1980s have made their peace with him.

Dole's greatest political weakness (or is it his greatest strength?) is his allergy to ideas. He mistrusts them, and he mistrusts people who have them. It's hard to imagine what a President Dole would spend his days doing—except, of course, for building a U.S. ethanol industry second to none. Even so, nobody could equal his power. One Republican compared the Dole presidential machine to the Red Army in its great days: maybe it's creaky and out of date, but nothing on earth can match its mass and firepower.

If Dole disdains ideology, Lamar Alexander is attempting to transcend it. He had originally planned to run on a platform of congressional reform: "Cut their pay and send them home." That message, obviously, packs less punch among Republicans than it did before the 1994 election—so Alexander campaigned instead as an "outsider" against the Washington "insiders" Gramm and Dole. He hoped to attract party moderates with his friendly face and speaking style, while winning over conservatives by outlining big—though vague—changes in the way Washington does business.

On the face of it this would seem an unpromising strategy. Alexander, after all, served in the Bush Cabinet as Secretary of Education after two successful terms as a centrist pro-business governor of Tennessee. Never before in his political career had he evidenced any sign of unhappiness with the way the United States is governed. But after 1992 he struck populist notes whenever he could, if not always on key. Visiting the lower-Manhattan editorial offices of the *Wall Street Journal* one August day to make his pitch, he arrived in a polo shirt and hiking boots, looking less like the Last Angry Man than like someone who had paid an image consultant $400 an hour to tell him how to dress up as Cincinnatus relinquishing the plough.

Any political consultant would have had to rank Dole or Alexander as safer political choices than Gramm. Their ideas were less radical, their visages less homely, their personalities less prickly. But, curiously, the staid Republican Party seems to be the party that pays less attention to safety. The roster of recent Democratic presidential candidates is gray with moderation and risk-aversion: Clinton, Dukakis, Mondale. It is the party of Reagan and Gingrich that is the adventuresome party, the party that thrills to political risk. Nominating Gramm would have been the biggest risk yet. Too bad for him that 1994 did not teach Republicans to trust their luck.

Pat Buchanan

The Conservative Bully Boy

Like the Lithuanian *bubbies* who haunt the stories of Philip Roth, embarrassing the young folks with Yiddish and garlic when they bring their gentile friends home, Patrick Buchanan is everything that couth conservatives want to escape. But the more you want *bubbie* to go away, the more determinedly she hangs around. Open the local tabloid and there is Buchanan defending a Nazi war criminal. Turn on the TV and there he is again, sputtering and going red in the face about the threat of colored immigration. Sort through the mail and there's his newsletter, bringing you the straight dope on how communism inspired the civil rights movement.

Of late, though, Buchanan's outbursts have been directed at an unusual target: conservatives whose conservatism differs from his own. Despite his vast material success, it seems, Buchanan is a man with a festering grievance: smart people, on the right as much as on the left, don't respect him. And, as readers of Buchanan's tough-guy memoir *Right from the Beginning* will recall, Buchanan knows only one thing to do with people who don't respect him: stomp them.

So in two May 1991 columns, Buchanan invited the panty-waists, bookworms, and wiseacres in the conservative movement to step outside. "Before true conservatives can ever take back the country," he snarled in the first of the columns, "they are first going to have to take back their movement." From whom? He answered that question a week later in a second column: from the "neoconservatives . . . the ex-liberals, socialists, and Trotskyists who signed on in the name of anti-communism and now control our foundations and set the limits of permissible dissent."

The first column cited at length a book chapter by Paul Gottfried of Elizabethtown College, which appeared in the March
issue of a newsletter edited by Murray Rothbard and Llewellyn
Rockwell of the Ludwig von Mises Institute. Buchanan darkly
observed "the capture of the four big conservative foundations by
neo-con staffers who are steering $30 million a year to front
groups, magazines, scholars and policy institutions who toe their
party line."

The party line these mysteriously powerful people enforce is
subverting what Buchanan understands as true conservatism:

> Ex-Great Society liberals, almost all of them, they support the
> welfare state and Big Government. They are pro-civil rights and
> affirmative action, though anti-quota. They are pro-foreign aid,
> especially for Israel. They favor higher immigration quotas; and
> some demand open borders.
>
> Many are viscerally hostile to the Old Right, and to any
> America First foreign policy. They want to use America's wealth
> to promote "global democracy" abroad and impose "democratic
> values" in our public schools.
>
> While they supported Reagan against Carter, their heroes are
> Woodrow Wilson and FDR, globalists and architects of the mam-
> moth modern state. Though most neo-cons were opposed to
> America's war in Vietnam, they were wildly pro-war against
> Iraq—even in August [1990].

Buchanan endorses the withering opinion of these conservatives held by Tom Fleming, editor of the Rockford Institute's
Chronicles magazine: "They have a lock on all money and the
institutions created by the right; they have established a cozy
relationship with the leftist establishment media who recognize
them for what they are, well-groomed lap dogs who bark but
never bite."

In the second column, Buchanan lamented that Reagan-era
conservativism had ended in failure. "Conservatives today cheer a
regime that spends a record 25 percent of the GNP, that is using
our wealth to erect a Wilsonian New World Order, that has given
us two wars, a tax increase and a dramatic increase in state
power." He blamed this dismal situation not on a free-spending
Congress, nor on a namby-pamby President, but on the true right's
fatal dalliance with neoconservatism.

> The postwar Old Right came together to roll back the New Deal, to dismantle the welfare-warfare state of FDR. Today's new "conservatism," by whatever fancy name it is called, is devoted to Big Government, minority rights and globalism.

With grim satisfaction Buchanan concluded, "The new battle for the American right has been joined."

It's been opened, at least. It can't be fully joined until there's a little more candor about who's on which side and what the fight's about.

Buchanan is being uncandid, first, because the litmus tests he has borrowed from Gottfried, Rothbard, and *Chronicles* to distinguish good, true conservatives from bad neoconservatives are not very useful. Is Richard Nixon—who considered Woodrow Wilson the greatest of twentieth-century Presidents—now a neoconservative? Is Jack Kemp—pro-Israel, pro-globalism, pro-immigration, pro–civil rights—another? Could it possibly be that Ronald Reagan—himself pro-Israel, pro-globalism, pro-immigration, pro–civil rights, and, on top of everything else, pro-FDR—is a third?

And what is this anti-neoconservative position that Buchanan is summoning his admirers to? What decent person is *against* "civil rights"? Who wouldn't be "viscerally hostile" to a capital A, capital F "America First" policy—a policy that as late as the dangerous summer and fall of 1941 denied that a Nazi-dominated Europe from Moscow to Madrid was anything the United States ought to be bothered by?

There is in fact nothing particularly "neoconservative" about the pro-internationalism, pro-immigration, pro-democracy ideological position Buchanan has set himself against. You'll find it espoused at the Heritage Foundation and on the editorial page of the *Wall Street Journal,* in the University of Chicago faculty lounge and—yes, Mr. Rockwell—in the pages of Ludwig von Mises.

Buchanan is uncandid, second, because so many of the anti-neoconservative grievances he airs are pure flimflam. Buchanan's pals at Rockford, for instance, never tire of repeating the legend that their quarrel with people they label "neoconservatives" erupted when Irving Kristol, whom they consider the Gavrilo Princip of the conflict, persuaded President-elect Reagan not to nominate the historian M. E. Bradford to the chairmanship of the National Endowment for the Humanities. The job was given to Kristol's friend William Bennett instead.

But the legend is false. By his own admission, Edwin Feulner of the Heritage Foundation (who never in his life had a good word to say for the Great Society) was much more instrumental than Kristol in kiboshing the Bradford appointment—and for the very good reason that Bradford, although a fine mind and a graceful writer, had published essays that could reasonably be understood by an unfriendly reader to liken Abraham Lincoln to Hitler. It's expecting rather a lot to ask a newly elected President to wreck his political honeymoon in order to refight the Civil War.★

The willingness of the sort of conservatives who congregate at *Chronicles* and around Patrick Buchanan to take offense at such insubstantial slights can best be explained ecologically. Since the early 1980s, the environment has grown more competitive for conservatives: their numbers are booming and their predators are growing steadily more skillful. Ecological crisis causes aggression in white mice, and, as any cancer researcher can tell you, Man is just a big, hairless white mouse.

But silly and self-interested as the people who articulate them may be, genuine internecine quarrels do exist in conservatism: How big a government should conservatives be prepared to live with? How adventurous a foreign policy is compatible with limited government? How much mutual cooperation can be expected from the various conservative factions?

It is indeed true, as Buchanan says, that quite a number of influential and visible conservatives have shown a dismaying willingness to throw in the towel on the Big Government issue. Fred Barnes identified John Sununu, William Bennett, Jack Kemp, and Dan Quayle as the Bush administration's leading Big Government conservatives. In Congress, Newt Gingrich and Jesse Helms throw money at their favored constituencies with nearly as much abandon as their opponents across the floor. Journalists like Irving Kristol in his occasional columns in the *Wall Street Journal* and Jude Wanniski in the editorials he wrote for the paper in the 1970s have warned Republicans against excessive preoccupation with budget-

---

★Gottfried repeats even more often the weird allegation that he himself lost a tenured appointment at Catholic University of America because a very junior faculty member named Jerry Z. Muller told the university authorities that Gottfried was "anti-Zionist"—at the behest, Gottfried believes, of Norman Podhoretz. If the story is true, the only thing more astonishing than Podhoretz's sway over the Catholic Church is Catholic University's amazingly respectful treatment of its junior faculty.

cutting. Many foreign-policy conservatives—both political figures like Jeane Kirkpatrick and Max Kampelman and commentators like Abe Rosenthal and Charles Krauthammer—seem willing, or even eager, to live with a meddlesome state at home as the price of an activist government abroad. Some of these conservatives attach the "neo" prefix to their politics; others don't. Buchanan's warnings against forgetting that American conservatism is, first and foremost, about limited government should be heeded by all of them.

If only he remembered to heed them himself. Buchanan's taste for limited government and free markets is as inconsistent as any ex-Trotskyist's. Like the blast-furnace left, he's suspicious of economic activity he finds hard to understand. In April 1990 he complained:

> What have the vulture capitalists of the leveraged buyout left us but an endless pile of clippings from *Women's Wear Daily* of their grinning selves and painted women? . . . As Germany and Japan capture markets once held by the United States, the predators slash R&D to paint up the profit-and-loss statement for the lenders; and the hell with the future.

As Greg Jarrell of the University of Rochester and Steve Kaplan of the University of Chicago have amply documented, the "vulture capitalists" have left us, along with the usual human quotient of mistakes and bad deals, a corporate economy that is considerably more efficient and profitable than it was ten years ago.

Buchanan has trouble, too, in grasping Adam Smith's and David Ricardo's lesson that we prosper when foreigners do. His faith in free enterprise peters out at the water's edge. On May 18, 1990, he fretted:

> Does free trade make for the efficient allocation of resources? Undoubtedly. But if the efficient allocation of resources means America's unskilled go jobless, while Mexico's unskilled get work, why not come down on the side of American workers? . . . A foreign policy that looks out for America First should be married to an economic policy that considers first the well-being of our own workers.

Nor is Buchanan a consistent small-government man on non-economic topics. One of the greatest intrusions of state power into private life during the Reagan and Bush years—the war on drugs and the concomitant enlargement of federal powers to seize assets and scrutinize financial transactions—has escaped his censure.

Another of Buchanan's challenges to the mainstream of contemporary conservatism, his isolationism, might also have been a
needed corrective—if only it didn't have the same now-you-see-it,
now-you-don't quality as his opposition to Big Government. There
are conservatives who recklessly set no limits on the scope for
American activity overseas, who can't pronounce the word "interest" without prefacing it with the word "vital." They ought to be
reproved. But Buchanan, who argued for six months against President Bush's determination to use all possible means to eject Saddam Hussein from Kuwait, spent the first half of January denouncing the President's refusal to use all possible means to eject the
Soviets from the Baltic republics. When Soviet tanks entered
Lithuania the week before the beginning of the air war against Iraq,
Buchanan thundered, "Are we with them [the Lithuanians], or
with Mikhail Gorbachev?" Indifference to the question of who
rules 40 percent of the world's known oil reserves is, in Buchanan's
mind, chest-thumping nationalism, but indifference to the question
of who rules downtown Vilnius is appeasement of a brutal dictatorship. And while Saddam Hussein—poison gas and all—was,
according to the great isolationist, someone the world could live
with, the Sandinistas in sleepy Nicaragua and the Marxist government of distant Angola were imminent threats to the security of the
Free World.

There is, however, one bone that Buchanan has to pick with
other conservatives that he never lays aside: his determination to
preserve the present ethnocultural character of the U.S.—or, better
yet, to return to the ethnocultural character that prevailed before
the social revolutions of the 1960s. Nicholas Lemann's book *The
Promised Land* quotes a March 1970 note of John Ehrlichman's,
which records President Nixon saying of his then-speechwriter:
"No good politics in PB's [Patrick Buchanan's] extreme view: segregation forever." Twenty years later, Martin Luther King's name
still makes Buchanan twitch. "Many liberals," Buchanan wrote in
November, "now insist that King's conservative critics bend the
knee, pay homage, honor him with a holiday, or be dismissed as
bigots. Good for Arizona for rejecting this hypocrisy."

Now, the preservation of the existing ethnocultural character of
the United States is not in itself an illegitimate goal. Shorn of
Buchanan's more unhygienic rhetoric, and with the emphasis on
culture rather than ethnicity, it's a goal that many conservatives

share. If anything, a concern that the ethnocultural character of the United States is being changed in unwholesome ways is the quality that distinguishes the conservativism of *Commentary* and the *Public Interest* from the more economically minded conservatism that pervades the Washington think tanks. But there does come a point— it's not always precisely indicated, but most of us know where it is—where ethnocultural conservatism shades into Kook-land.

Kook-land is a terrain that every journalist has seen. Some journalists, though, get to know it better than others. They take a little more care reading the long, handwritten letters from paranoid readers. They weigh the charges of conspiracy a little more thoughtfully. They write back a little more promptly. And the inhabitants of Kook-land have a curious power to anticipate which journalists will be friendliest to them. Almost clairvoyantly, they detect the gnawing resentments, the hidden status anxiety, the carefully concealed sense of unrewarded merit that renders journalists susceptible to the Call of the Kooky.

Normally, highly successful and well-paid journalists are the most immune to Kookery. Not Buchanan. The man's opinions are carried by a hundred newspapers and two networks, PBS and CNN. He has replaced George Will and William F. Buckley as the most visible conservative in the country. He earns an income of half a million a year. Ans still he's an easy mark for every Holocaust-denial nut in the country.

So, while the questions of the appropriate size of government, the appropriate reach of U.S. foreign policy, and the appropriate rate of change in the ethnocultural character of the United States all matter, the question that matters most in the recurring Buchanan controversies is an easier one: How deeply into kookery can a man who claims to speak for conservatism go before other conservatives are obliged to repudiate him?

This is a question bigger than any one personality, however notorious. It is a question whose answer will tell a lot about whether conservatism after Reagan is to be a real alternative to the political status quo, or merely a protest movement.

While conservatives have been more or less in charge of the executive branch for more than a decade, they have not enjoyed much success in reducing the burden of government. Conservatives have suffered that lack of success not because they have entered into compromising alliances with "ex-Trotskyists" who complacently accept Big Government, but because they have failed to win control of Congress, the branch of government that actually decides how much of the taxpayers' money Washington will spend.

There are three possible responses to this failure. One is to embrace the Big Government conservatism that Buchanan execrates. Another is to effect institutional reforms—term limits, new parliamentary rules in Congress, a balanced budget amendment, a line-item veto that would impose discipline on Congress's spending. A third is to try harder to elect Republicans to Congress, in the hope that a Republican-controlled legislature would be less spendthrift.

Electing a Republican Congress will require coalition-building. Coalition-building, in turn, requires a certain etiquette. The members of an electoral coalition do not have to like each other. They certainly do not need to be of one mind on fundamental philosophical principles. But they do have to agree on what should be done tomorrow morning. If some conservatives continue to think that the highest priority remains what it was—a reduction in the burden of government—while others have come to feel that the present burden is perfectly tolerable so long as the right people are in charge of it, then the conservative coalition is, as Buchanan says, dead.

Small Government, though, is hardly Buchanan's real message, as the inconsistency of his writing about it shows. Neither is a more modest foreign policy. His real message is inseparable from his sly Jew-baiting and his not-so-sly gay-bashing, from his old record as a segregationist and his current maunderings about immigrants and the Japanese. And it's not a message that can be accommodated in any conservatism—Big Government or Small—that seriously hopes to govern a great and diverse country. In fact, it's exactly the kind of message that William F. Buckley thought he had purged from American conservatism back in the 1950s and early 1960s, when he chased Gerald L. K. Smith and the John Birchers away from *National Review*. The time has come to chase it away again. This exclusion will not disappoint Buchanan very much, since actually governing the country is about the last thing that his sort of conservatism has in mind.

Good-bye Pat

In an increasingly conservative America, one political figure defiantly resists the historical tide. This man still denounces big banks and multinational corporations. Still unabashedly puts the interests of the American factory worker ahead of those of the so-called international trading system. Still refuses even to contemplate any cuts in the generosity of big middle-class spending programs like Medicare and Social Security. This man is Patrick Buchanan: America's last leftist.

On the airwaves it is Buchanan whose ads attack the House Republicans' Medicare reform and accuse his party of cutting off elderly Americans in order to aid the already privileged. As he told ABC's Cokie Roberts in October 1995, "Their [the Republicans'] priorities are wrong. Why didn't they go after foreign aid? Why didn't they go after this $50 billion Mexican bailout which is unraveling before our eyes?"

In his campaign speeches, Buchanan bluntly blames the falling wages of laborers like "the single mom in a textile plant in South Carolina" on "investment bankers on Wall Street" who want her "to compete with Asian workers who have to work for twenty-five cents an hour."

While Democrats nervously ingratiate themselves with corporate donors, Buchanan roars his hostility to big business. In the *Wall Street Journal,* he blasted "multinational corporations whose loyalty is only to the bottom line on a balance sheet"; and suggested the U.S. government "inform these amoral behemoths they are welcome to bring in their capital and build their plants. But if they shut down factories here to open overseas, they will pay a price for the readmission of their goods to the American market."

Measured by the traditional New Deal standards—which candidate attacks corporations most violently? which candidate opposes reductions in government most strenuously?—Buchanan has moved to the left of President Clinton. Hey, he's moved to the left of virtually *every* Democrat now holding national office.

Does that sound implausible? Look at the world for a moment through the eyes of a union organizer. The intense new international competition in manufacturing has forced American companies to be less tolerant of impediments to the efficient use of labor—i.e., you. Which presidential candidate is promising to shut that competition down and put you back in the driver's seat? Only Pat Buchanan, who has called for a 40-percent tariff on Chinese exports, a 20-percent tariff on Japanese goods, and an unspecified "social tariff" on exports from Third World countries.

Now imagine yourself an embittered, downwardly mobile ex-autoworker. Who speaks to your grievances more directly than

Buchanan, who laments a "burnt out Detroit, once the forge of the Great Arsenal of Democracy, . . . ghost towns that were once factory towns, . . . the stagnant wages of an alienated working class and a middle class newly introduced to insecurity"?

Or put yourself in the shoes of a marginal Southern tobacco farmer, fearful of what NAFTA and global agricultural trade liberalization will do to his no-longer guaranteed home market. Who is offering a more convincing solution to your problems than Buchanan with his attacks on trade deals cooked up in order "to ship Mexico tens of billions to pay off its creditors at Citibank and Goldman Sachs?"

The party of Franklin Delano Roosevelt now represents a coalition of blacks, working women, public employees, trial lawyers, college professors, and high-tech industry. The party long ago turned its back on the dwindling remains of President Roosevelt's original farmer-labor-white ethnic coalition. It's a constituency without a voice, and Buchanan is cleverly attempting to speak for it. No doubt, Buchanan enlivens his Rooseveltian politics with some spicy condiments all his own. The adoption of the sinister term "New World Order" to describe what is in fact a half-century-old bipartisan free-trade policy is distinctively Buchanan-esque, as is the habit of using Jewish names to personify the things he dislikes. (The investment bankers Mr. Buchanan rails against consistently work for Goldman Sachs, never Morgan Stanley or Bear Stearns.)

True too, Buchanan advocates a program of flatter and lower taxes on income and capital that mix uncomfortably with his anti-corporate rhetoric: the elimination of inheritance taxes on estates of less than $5 million, for instance. A vestigial Goldwaterism likewise manifests itself in Buchanan's continued championing of the old social-conservative single-issue causes: guns, abortion, prayer in the schools.

But even so, compare the Pat Buchanan of today to the Pat Buchanan of 1992. The core issue of Buchanan's primary challenge to President Bush was the *echt*-Reaganite accusation that Mr. Bush had backslid on taxes. Even the notorious speech to the 1992 Republican convention—for all its abandonment of the sunny and generous tone characteristic of Ronald Reagan—bashed Governor Clinton for his indifference to foreign policy, his pro-choice views on abortion, his sympathy to gay rights, his opposition to school choice, and the free-spending ways of running-mate Al Gore. All orthodox Reagan doctrines.

Today, Buchanan still forthrightly states his views on abortion and gay rights—if asked. But his campaign speeches stress arresting new themes: the imminent menace of world government, the greed of international banks, the power of tariffs to stop the deterioration in blue-collar wages, the urgency of preserving Medicare in something close to its present form. This isn't anything remotely like the conservative Republicanism of the Reagan era. What it sounds very much like instead is the militant, resentful rhetoric roared by populist Democrats from William Jennings Bryan onward.

The revulsion contemporary Democrats feel for Buchanan only exposes how far that party has drifted from its own past. After all, on the issues contemporary Democrats really care about—abortion, affirmative action, the environment—big business can often be counted on to cooperate with reasonable grace. The resentments that modern Democrats attempt to appeal to are increasingly racial or sexual ("They just don't get it") rather than economic.

But there's no reason to expect that economic resentment will remain a taboo forever. It's often said that in good economic times people are willing to tolerate redistribution, but in bad times they hunker down. Maybe. But put aside the 1960s, and you see another pattern. During the other prosperous decades of the century—the 1920s, the 1950s, the 1980s—Americans have trusted in the fairness of their economic system and ignored complaints that the game is rigged. When good jobs are plentiful, voters tend to believe, not unreasonably, that the way to get ahead is to go out and work. It's in bad times—the 1930s, the 1970s—that voters grumble against big business and big banks. It's in bad times that voters elect politicians who offer them quack nostrums to create jobs.

And for one big category of workers—high school–educated men under age forty—times have been genuinely hard for nearly fifteen years. In them, a constituency for resentful economics has reappeared. So far, the politicians who have attempted to exploit this constituency have failed either because they were patent phonies (Richard Gephardt in 1988) or because they refused to reckon with these men's conservative racial views (Jesse Jackson in 1984 and 1988) or because they labored under the weight of too much standard-issue Democratic baggage (Tom Harkin in 1992). Buchanan suffers from none of these handicaps, and it may take him far.

The important question for traditional conservative Republicans is how far Buchanan should be permitted to take the party. The success of Buchanan's 1992 campaign has already begun to redirect the Republican party to a more restrictive position on immigration and a much harder line on affirmative action. More successes in 1996 will enhance his influence even more. Should he be welcomed or not?

In 1992, many conservatives suffered excruciating difficulty in deciding. Only a month after William F. Buckley concluded in a powerful cover story in *National Review* that he found it impossible to defend Buchanan against accusations of anti-Semitism, the editors of that same magazine urged a "tactical vote" for Buchanan in the New Hampshire primary. This time, though, the choice ought to be easier. Conservatives need to recognize that Buchanan's politics are neither a throwback to the Taft Republicanism of the 1930s and 1940s (Taft would have hacked up Medicare with gusto) nor a renovation of Reaganite conservatism for the post–Cold War world. It is something new: a populism formed to seize the political opportunities presented by strident multiculturalism and stagnating wages for less-skilled workers.

Populism, though, seldom offers answers to the problems it exploits. Cutting off immigration won't unify American culture. It is the alienation of black America from the country's old norms and ideals that is dividing the United States, and on that subject Buchanan has nothing to say.

Nor will restricting imports improve the lot of the less-skilled: tariffs are a tax that weighs most crushingly on the poorest people in society. The apogee of American protectionism—the years from the enactment of the McKinley tariff of 1890 to Woodrow Wilson's turn to free trade in 1913—were the years marked by the most extreme income inequality and the most violent labor strife in the nation's history.

As things are going, it is likely only a matter of time before Buchanan himself recognizes the rapidly mounting distance between his politics and those of mainstream conservatism. His friend and fellow-columnist Sam Francis, whose ideas Buchanan has increasingly echoed, has already dropped the self-description. The danger is not so much that Buchanan will hijack conservatism, as that even after he charges out of it on his way toward some unscouted ideological destination of his own, his statist and populist ideas will seep backward into it.

Buchanan has never shied from a fight, and neither should those Republicans who oppose him. Republicans who hold fast to the traditions of postwar conservatism that Buchanan is rejecting—small government and American global leadership—should make clear that they understand as well as Buchanan does the immense difference between his politics and theirs. He has turned his back on the fundamental convictions that have defined American conservatism for forty years, and conservatives shouldn't be afraid to say so. After all, to paraphrase Ronald Reagan, it isn't we who have left Pat Buchanan; it is Pat Buchanan who is leaving us.

Beyond Kemp

Look into the closets and back drawers of the Republicans supporting Phil Gramm, Dan Quayle, or Lamar Alexander for president in 1996, and you'll almost certainly find a "Jack Kemp for President" button. What enthusiasm that man once excited among conservatives! Everything they had wished the dreary old GOP of Gerald Ford and Bob Michel to be, he was—dynamic, charming, unashamedly pro-market, unquestionably big-hearted. When he walked into a room, he lit it up.

He transcended the party's internal divisions and contradictions. He was pro-life and pro-Israel, pro-gold standard and pro-Social Security, anticommunist and antiapartheid. He was "Yitzhak Kemp," an "AFL-CIO conservative," a "progressive conservative," an "Abraham Lincoln conservative." Seldom has a politician breathed more certainty that all Americans shared a common interest, that the hard money and low taxes that sent the Dow Jones average soaring would also enrich hardware store owners, beauticians, and oil refinery workers.

It was Kemp who sponsored and championed the most important single piece of conservative domestic legislation of the 1970s, the Kemp-Roth cut in marginal tax rates. It was Kemp who argued most passionately for locating the 1980 Republican convention in Detroit, to underscore the party's determination to win blue-collar and black votes. And at that convention, eager conservatives festooned themselves with "Reagan/Kemp" stickers, hoping against hope that Ronald Reagan would select the dynamic young congressman from Buffalo—not the colorless preppy from Greenwich—to fill the vice presidential slot, and (in the fullness of time) inherit the Oval Office.

It all seems quite incredible now.

In February 1995, after months of bad news from former supporters and contributors, Kemp announced his withdrawal from the 1996 race, and thus, at least for the present, from active politics. What went wrong?

The simplest answer is Kemp himself—his repeated refusal to take the risk of running for higher office, his loquacity, his unwillingness to learn from experience. It's easy to tick off his political misjudgments, culminating in the worst of them all—the failure to resign from the Bush cabinet in the summer of 1990 over the breaking of the "no new taxes" pledge and to run for governor of New York against a vulnerable Mario Cuomo. A Governor Kemp who remained faithful to his tax-cutting principles after George Bush had betrayed them—he could have burbled as loquaciously as he liked and still have been unbeatable in 1996.

But Kemp's rivals suffer their share of personality faults too. Why were Kemp's fatal when theirs were not?

Jack Kemp seemed to pride himself on refusing to change with the times. The speeches he gives today can barely be distinguished from those he gave seventeen years ago. Kemp is a political Dorian Grey, a man untouched by time even as everything around him is transformed by it.

As social order collapsed in the inner cities, Kemp kept promoting the same two pet nostrums that he imported from Margaret Thatcher's Britain in the late 1970s, tenant ownership of public housing and enterprise zones, despite accumulating evidence that they will not work.

Enterprise zones have not yet had an opportunity to fail in America, although they have been tested and found wanting across the Atlantic. But as secretary of housing and urban development under President Bush, Kemp had a chance to try his tenant ownership idea. The cost was huge—in just four years, Kemp upped his department's budget by 50 percent, from $19 billion to $27 billion—and the results were meager. Tenant ownership mutated almost instantly into yet another hideous bureaucracy under yet another deceptive acronym: HOPE, or Home Ownership for People Everywhere.

The privatization of public housing made Tories out of a wide swath of the British working class. But only 2 percent of Americans live in public housing, and they are overwhelmingly drawn from the ranks of welfare recipients, not workers. They are much less likely than their British counterparts to possess the cash to buy their homes (even at concessionary prices) and the skills to maintain them. Since American projects are vastly more violent, unattractive, and deteriorated places than the British, and since superior private-sector housing is available relatively cheaply, those tenants who do amass a bit of cash are going to want to leave, not buy.

Kemp's effort to apply the noncomparable British experience in the U.S. led to one of the strangest episodes in the history of the American welfare state, the Kenilworth-Parkside HOPE demonstration project. Kemp spent an average of $125,000 per apartment to renovate Kenilworth-Parkside. He then "sold" the units to the tenants on conditions that required them to put no money down and that precluded them from reselling their apartments on the open market, so as to prevent profiteering. To get HOPE through Congress, Kemp even had to promise to build one new unit of public housing for every unit sold.

In other words, HOPE—the very program that was supposed to replace state ownership of housing—ended up multiplying and entrenching it. Kemp had become so infatuated with tenant ownership that he traded away its substance to preserve the slogan.

This was more than mere obstinacy. Kemp believed, believed passionately, that the urban black poor were people pretty much like other Americans. If they seemed sunk in dependency and self-destructive behavior, the blame ought not to attach to some "culture of poverty" or to the bell curve, but to the perverse incentives of the welfare state. Yet Kemp until the very last weeks of his presidential hopes refused to come out for what he condemned as "punitive" Charles Murray–style reforms of that welfare state. The only escape from the dilemma was to roll back the welfare state in a way that didn't actually deprive any beneficiary of its benefits—in other words, HOPE.

Kemp never fully reckoned with the horror and fear that the destructive behavior of the urban underclass provoked in the American middle class—or in his party. Kemp's conservatism envisaged a little tinkering with the mechanism of government that would ignite economic growth and liberate the dormant entrepreneurial energies of the poor. Conservatism, 1990s-style, takes a far grimmer and more pessimistic attitude, and Kemp's happy-talk sounded increasingly anachronistic and naive.

For all the boldness of his language, for all his fondness for the word "revolution," Kemp never completely broke with the orthodoxies of postwar American liberalism. In the early Reagan years he clashed with David Stockman over the need for sizable spending cuts, and he lambasted Federal Reserve Board chairman Paul Volcker for raising interest rates to squeeze out the Carter inflation. Kemp didn't want to cut taxes in order to shrink the government— at least, he seldom said so. He wanted, he insisted, to cut taxes in order to *support* government. Kempism often sounded suspiciously like a deal with liberalism: if you put me in charge of the revenue side of the ledger, you can run the expenditure side as you please.

Up to a point, Kemp was right: The lowering of marginal income tax rates between 1981 and 1990 triggered a 50-percent increase in personal income tax collections over those years. But not even the abundant revenues of the Reagan years could keep pace with the extravagant spending commitments made by the Johnson and Nixon administrations.

As they grappled with the deficits spawned by the escalating costs of federal social welfare programs, more and more conservatives began to wonder whether the stodgy old Republicans overshadowed by Kemp in the 1970s hadn't been right—whether it wasn't government spending, after all, that was the core problem of modern government. If so, opposition to Big Government would have to be reincorporated as the defining doctrine of modern conservatism—leaving very little place in the movement for expansive, expensive Jack Kemp.

If Kemp's withdrawal from the presidential race signals a new determination among Republicans to cut the federal government down to size, then it is welcome. All the same, those of us who once wore his button on our lapels could not help feeling sad at his departure from the race. No other conservative leader is as untinctured by the small, the petty, the mean as Kemp. There was always something great and generous about the man. If his policies were credulous or misconceived, his determination that Republicans offer hope to the poor too was noble and right.

His most recent fight exemplified all that is best in him. Kemp could have preserved a discreet silence over California's Proposition 187, a law that (among other things) cuts off schooling to the children of illegal aliens. He could have concentrated his attention on his points of agreement with Californians unhappy about high levels of immigration to their state. He did neither. Kemp has championed immigration throughout his career, and he declined to change his mind at the end—even if it cost him his last hope of the presidency. Jointly with Bill Bennett (who had earlier inclined to favor 187), he defiantly published his opposition to the measure, and campaigned against it. At HUD, Kemp stubbornly refused to budge on tactics; that same stubbornness was a strength when he defended a point of principle. Kemp's problem was that he often had trouble telling the difference.

Perhaps the future will remember Jack Kemp only as we remember James G. Blaine, the most popular Republican of the 1880s and yet a man who never quite made the historical cut. But it would be more just if Kemp carried out with him an appellation he well deserves, the same appellation Dean Acheson applied to Harry Truman—"the captain with the mighty heart."

Dead Wrong

The spasm of worry and indignation about the resurgence of the Christian right ought to provoke an awkward question: If the Christian right is so powerful and well-organized, why does it nearly always lose?

Sure, Christian conservatives score the occasional electoral success, winning school board seats, assembly races, local Republican party chairmanships. But when they venture into bigger races, they get clobbered. Pat Robertson dropped out of the 1988 Republican presidential contest after finishing fourth in God-fearing South Carolina. The 1993 Republican landslide in Virginia failed to sweep home-schooler Mike Farris into the lieutenant governorship. Even Oliver North—who drew strength from non-evangelicals too—lost his 1994 Senate race to a very vulnerable Democrat.

The Christian right has not done much better wielding power indirectly. Has there been a network news report sympathetic to its point of view? What large corporation worries about its image in the evangelical community? How many senators and governors regard it as anything more than a nuisance to be managed?

You don't read this version of events in the papers because Christian conservatives and their detractors share an interest in hyping the movement's power. How else could People for the American Way scare up donors? It would be wiser, though, to take a more cold-eyed reading of the Christian right's flurry of publicity. To cast your eye down the roster of the movement's core issues is to survey a long series of defeats.

Separation of church and state. Six Reagan-Bush Supreme Court justices later, the establishment clause stands exactly as it did at the apogee of Warren Court liberalism. Baby Jesus and the farm animals must still keep off the courthouse square at Christmas. Students may not pray out loud in class; nor may Bibles be displayed.

In 1992 the Rehnquist Court went a step beyond even the Warren Court and ruled that a non-sectarian invocation by a Reform rabbi at a high school graduation violated the First Amendment. In fact, in the fifteen years since the founding of the Moral Majority, Christian conservatives have managed to poke only one brick out of the wall separating church and state: a 1984 opinion by Warren Burger permitted Christmas crèches on public property so long as they were accompanied by Frosty the Snowman or other secular seasonal symbols.

Curricula. School systems notoriously ignore parents' wishes, but few parents have suffered so complete a dismissal as Christian conservatives. The demand for school choice—seen by some secular liberals as yet another offensive in the Christian right's assault on the Constitution—actually reflects evangelicals' despair that the schools they help pay for will ever heed their wishes. Attempts to introduce "creation science" alongside evolution in science classes were squelched by the Reaganized Supreme Court in 1987. Meanwhile, at the state level, education reformers have pushed schools to devote more energy to teaching science, including evolutionary biology. Publishers, leery of getting caught in denominational crossfires, have expunged references to religion from their history textbooks. Comparative religion classes, which many districts substituted for Bible-reading in the '60s and '70s, skip by Martin Luther and John Wesley on their way to the wisdom of the Hopi.

Christian conservatives do sometimes score an educational point: witness the shooting down of New York state's pro-gay Rainbow Curriculum. But how impressive was that victory really? If a curricular innovation is also opposed by Roman Catholics and observant Jews, and if it goes so far that it makes even secular conservatives queasy, and if it also happens to reflect black nationalism at its most chauvinist, and if large sectors of the electorate are already annoyed at the schools' chancellor for bungling an asbestos cleanup—why, then, you can chalk up yet another big win for those fearsome Christians.

Obscenity. Not so very long ago, it used to be difficult to watch a dirty movie in America. Now pay-per-view T.V. beams them into every rumpus room and business hotel. How free is the sort of speech disliked by the Christian right? Three years ago the country was riven by a controversy over the National Endowment for the Arts: should taxpayers have to pay naked women to smear themselves with chocolate? Should a crucifix submerged in urine collect government money when no other crucifix could? The answer to both questions: Yes. All the NEA artists blackballed by the Bush Administration have jumped back on the public payroll. If the Christian right couldn't win that one, it can't win anything.

Abortion. After twenty-one years of the bitterest ideological struggle perhaps since slavery, abortion retains its status as a constitutionally guaranteed right—a right reaffirmed twice by the Reagan-era Supreme Court in its *Webster* and *Casey* decisions. It's early yet to declare a winner, but certainly the pro-choice side is way ahead on points: though it is indisputably tougher to obtain an abortion in America today than in 1977, 1.5 million are still performed every year. Violent attacks on abortion doctors and clinics only confirm the triumph of the pro-choice cause. Supporters of legalized abortion shun violence because they know they're winning; like the student radicals of the early 1970s, pro-life fanatics turn to violence because they sense they are losing.

Gay Rights. When Anita Bryant of orange juice fame launched her jeremiad against homosexuality in the mid-1970s, conservative evangelicals appeared to have discovered the perfect issue. Here was a tiny minority living in ways that the overwhelming majority had in those days been raised to recoil from. Here, if anywhere, the Christian right should have been able to rally Americans to roll back the advance of sexual modernism. Instead, the transformation of the legal and social status of homosexuality over the following years brutally exposed the weakness of Christian social conservatism. The American Civil Liberties Union counts more than one hundred jurisdictions, ranging from the state of California to the town of Yellow Springs, Ohio, that have extended legal protection to homosexuality or gay domestic partnerships since 1977.

It's not surprising that a moral revaluation of this magnitude should have provoked opposition. What's surprising is how spotty the opposition has been. Conservatives eked out a compromise on the gays in the military fight and carried a Colorado referendum on gay rights—a referendum that now looks unlikely to survive judicial review. But in many other places, steadily and surely, the gay rights cause is carrying the day.

Christian conservatives often react with hostility to bad news, even when they hear it from their friends. Good populists, they confuse the observation that they *are* losing with the opinion that they *ought* to lose. And they usually reply to bad news by citing polling data that indicate substantial public support for their positions.

In this, however, Christian conservatives are again betrayed by their populism. It's one thing for the general public to entertain a belief; quite another to turn that belief into law. American politics is a far more elitist business than most of us are comfortable admitting. In the long months between elections, public policy is made by bureaucracies, legislatures, and courts. Public opinion is like the atomic bomb in international relations: useful when it comes time for the ultimate showdown, but not terribly relevant to ordinary decision-making. More important than the ability to pack a nomination meeting in Amarillo is the ability to sway the media, to attract support in the academic world, to lobby congressional staffers, to write a solid legal brief.

To do those things requires skills that Christian conservatives generally lack. Perhaps because the theological liberals scooped up the best divinity schools and richest congregations in the great schism of the early twentieth century, or perhaps because contemporary evangelicalism puts so much emphasis on emotion rather than doctrine, the evangelical church is a decapitated institution. It fulfills the spiritual yearnings of millions, but it has trouble justifying itself to scoffers and doubters. Henry Ward Beecher, the great mid-nineteenth-century evangelist, commanded the respect even of his antagonists. Pat Robertson doesn't.

In the past, Christian conservatives have compensated for their lack of sophistication by accepting the leadership of secular politicians such as Ronald Reagan. It is understandable that many of them have come to reject that strategy: once elected, their allies often turn out to care more about tort reform than godliness. But because they lack effective leadership of their own, breaking ranks with secular conservatives either leaves Christian conservatives marshaled behind evangelical enthusiasts who alienate non-evangelicals (like Farris) or vulnerable to cunning outsiders with agendas of their own (like North).

Not So
Wild About Harry

In October 1995, several hundred of the sort of people Harry Truman would likely have cursed as "bloodsuckers" on one of his intemperate days paid upwards of $1,000 per ticket to attend a black-tie fundraiser in Washington, D.C., for the Truman Library. The dinner was just one of a series of events commemorating the fiftieth anniversary of Harry Truman's ascension to the presidency in April 1945. The anniversary committee was chaired by all the living presidents, and President and Mrs. Clinton were the guests of honor.

These anniversary celebrations cap a spectacular posthumous rehabilitation of the thiry-first president, a rehabilitation now brought to television by a hagiographic Home Box Office film. President Clinton has lavished praise on David McCullough's loving 1992 biography of Truman. When challenged on his decision to admit uncloseted homosexuals into the military, Clinton cited Truman's equally controversial desegregation of the armed forces. The president—like all trailing incumbents—apparently is taking the desperate, come-from-behind 1948 campaign as a model for his own reelection.

Nor is it merely partisan Democrats who honor Truman. Ronald Reagan and his neoconservative allies also claimed to have been inspired by Harry Truman, humble populist and steely anticommunist. Who remembers now that Truman left office in near-disgrace? A country victorious in the Cold War salutes the author of the Truman doctrine and the champion of the Marshall Plan. A country weary of deceit in high places treasures the memory of Truman's bluntness, his strength of purpose, his confidence in

himself and the rightness of America's cause. Our Truman is the
Truman McCullough lionizes:

> He stood for common sense, common decency. He spoke the
> common tongue. As much as any president since Lincoln, he
> brought to the highest office the language and values of the com-
> mon American people. He held to the old guidelines: work hard,
> do your best, speak the truth, assume no airs, trust in God, have
> no fear. Yet he was not and had never been a simple, ordinary
> man. . . . He was the kind of president the founding fathers had
> in mind for the country.

And all of this is true. But so is this: Truman spent a week visiting Yale in 1958. At a meeting with a small group of faculty and
graduate students, the ex-president was asked how a southerner
like himself had come to support civil rights. Truman "replied elo-
quently that all Americans had fundamental rights. Then he added,
'But personally I don't care to associate with niggers.'"

That story comes from the 1995 biography of Truman by Professor Alonzo L. Hamby of Ohio University, an astringent corrective to the saccharine now served by Truman's uncritical admirers.
It is a book that should be read by everyone who prefers history to
mythmaking. Hamby believes that Truman was a great president,
as indeed he was. But he also reminds us that a great president is
not always a great man. Truman's cronyism, his violent temper, his
self-pity, his vacillation, his pettiness often justified the doubts of
his contemporaries about his fitness for high office. Hamby
observes that Truman "often felt suspicious of those around him,
was capable of considerable vindictiveness, seethed with unfocused
hostility, and, above all, dealt poorly with stress."

Truman's iconographers have endorsed George Marshall's
assessment of the "integrity of the man." McCullough describes an
ex-president who, though never wealthy, "was not for sale. He
would take no fees for commercial endorsements or for lobbying or
writing letters or making phone calls. He would accept no 'consult-
ing fees,' nor any gifts that might appear as a product endorsement
on his part." There is no entry for "corruption" in McCullough's
index.

Yet corruption was one of the trio of issues that sank the Democrats in 1952 (the others being Korea and communism). Between
Teapot Dome and Watergate, no administration was as severely

buffeted as Truman's by allegations of influence peddling, most of them true: government loans were directed to prominent Democrats and their friends, administration officials accepted gifts large and small, and old war-buddies of Truman's accumulated tidy fortunes as "five-per-centers." For the sake of his party, Truman was prepared to make all sorts of ethical compromises: in 1948, he fired the liberal head of the Civil Aeronautics Board, James M. Landis, under circumstances that lead Hamby to believe that he was motivated by the desire for campaign contributions from the aviation industry. Truman may have been an underdog in 1948, but he still raised considerably more money than his opponent, Governor Thomas E. Dewey: $2.7 million vs. $2.1 million. Nor, unlike, say Ulysses S. Grant, was Truman invariably personally scrupulous: as a senator, he had put his wife on his office payroll at a salary higher than any other of his employees—a practice condemned even by the loose ethical norms of the day.

Of course, if the only flaws marring Harry Truman's reputation were his personal flaws or his administration's improprieties, recalling them now would be ridiculously beside the point. What president or presidency has gone unscathed by those? Nobody should begrudge a few bouts of irascibility to the president who saved Western Europe from starvation and communism, who imposed democratic institutions on Germany and Japan, and who won the Korean War. Unfortunately, though, history records some far more significant debits in the ledger of Truman's achievements.

Alongside Truman's magnificent successes in foreign affairs, there lies an ominous record at home. All of us, on both sides of the Atlantic and Pacific, owe Truman thanks for the peaceful, secure, postcommunist world we live in. But whenever a contemporary president hails Truman as a model for our own time, we should keep it in mind that if conservative Congresses had not shot his domestic program to pieces, our peaceful, secure, postcommunist world would be a dramatically poorer one.

No American president ever proposed worse economic policies than Harry Truman. The great postwar economic boom that began in 1945 appalled and disgusted Truman, and he exerted all his political power in an attempt to shut it down. Truman wanted to impose a permanent war economy on the United States: a comprehensive system of wage, price and credit controls; state allocation of investment capital; and confiscatory taxation—all supervised by a bureaucracy left almost entirely to its own discretion. It could even be argued, in fact, that Truman's most important personal contribution to the nation's future prosperity was his unpopularity: dislike of him helped elect the conservative postwar Congresses that rejected statism at precisely the moment of its maximum prestige. It's more than a little frightening to imagine what the country might look like now if Harry Truman's program had won the backing of a beloved figure like General Eisenhower.

America returned to peace in 1945 in an anxious mood. The country was wracked by inflation and strikes. Unsurprisingly so. Since 1940, the Federal Reserve had let the printing presses rip. To prevent all that new currency from having its natural inflationary effect, the Roosevelt administration had established an elaborate system of price controls. Wartime enthusiasm eased the enforcement of the controls: it also helped that workers were pressured to invest their money in war bonds, locking up in savings accounts money that might otherwise have bid up the prices of goods.

The Truman administration had planned to finance postwar reconstruction the same way that the Roosevelt administration had financed the war: by continuing to print money, borrowing at very low rates, and suppressing price increases. The plan failed. With the war over, people stopped buying war bonds and started cashing them instead, in hopes of buying a few peacetime luxuries: new tires, beefsteaks, civilian clothes. Goods vanished from stores; prices shot upwards. In August 1945, Truman decontrolled wages, and the major unions immediately demanded huge raises, 30 percent and more. When balked, union leaders (some of them communist-inspired) began exploiting the awesome powers conferred on them by New Deal labor legislation. They yanked their followers out on strikes that threatened to shut the country down: rail strikes and steel strikes, auto strikes and coal strikes.

These strikes enraged Truman, and he took stern action to end them: in the case of the rail strike, he threatened to draft the strikers and subject them to military discipline unless they returned to work. But the only solution to the inflation and shortages problem that Truman could imagine was to redouble the policies that had created the problem in the first place: easy money and price controls. The president's authority to impose price controls expired in June 1946. In August, Congress restored price controls, but in a much weaker form. Truman never ceased demanding his wartime economic powers back.

Hamby grimly describes Truman's determination to institution-alize a command economy. In September 1946, Truman presented Congress with his first comprehensive postwar economic program: more controls on prices, a higher minimum wage, a law committing the Federal Reserve to easy money, a huge federal housing pro-gram, subsidies to small business, veterans' benefits, more generous Social Security payments, and a British-style national health insur-ance program. As he would do throughout his presidency, Truman proposed raising tax rates—already at wartime highs—as an anti-inflationary device. At the same time, recognizing that excessive taxation depressed economic production, he began punching loop-holes in the tax code to stimulate favored industries.

Truman's September program probably contributed as much as anything to the Republican landslide in November 1946. The reputation of the Eightieth Congress has been unjustly blackened by partisan historians. It was a Republican majority that enacted the Truman foreign policy. Republicans provided the aid to embat-tled Greece and Turkey demanded by the Truman doctrine and Republicans voted the funds for the Marshall Plan. Those same Republicans, though, rebelled against Truman's vision of a perma-nently militarized economy. Even before the Republican majority was sworn in, Truman unhappily abandoned most price controls; the new Congress scrapped the rest. Congress made short work too of most of his spending program, and twice sent him an unwanted tax cut, which he twice vetoed. Congress's repeal of price controls prompted the Federal Reserve to attack inflation by tightening money. As always, that worked. And the passage of the 1947 Taft-Hartley Act, curbing the wilder provisions of the 1935 Wagner Act, helped achieve labor peace.

But Truman's attachment to economic hokum did not waver. In November 1947, he proposed another Clement Atlee–style eco-nomic plan: controls on prices and consumer credit, federal alloca-tions of capital to industry, and rationing of consumer goods. Con-gress ignored him. Eight months later, Truman tried again. Everyone has heard of the famous "special session" of Congress convened by Truman in July 1948. He sent up obnoxious bill after bill, knowing that each would be rejected, justifying his claim that the eightieth was a "do nothing" Congress. Now take a look at the content of his bills: price controls again, a huge expansion of the federal housing program already transforming poor neighborhoods into nightmarish slums, national health insurance, federal support for and regulation of local school boards, and a renewed commitment to federal water projects to produce subsidized electricity. It was the Lyndon Johnson program, fifteen years early. And if we believe that Johnson's huge expansion of the federal government between 1965 and 1973 shut down the postwar expansion of the American economy, we ought to wonder: Would there have been a postwar economic expansion in the first place if Harry Truman's legislative program had succeeded?

Nor should the left-wing program of July 1948 be interpreted, as McCullough interprets it, as a mere tactic to split reasonable Dewey Republicans from the Taft mossbacks. Truman sincerely believed in it. After his re-election, he sent virtually the same set of policies up Capitol Hill again: repeal of Taft-Hartley, higher taxes, centrally planned hydroelectric authorities on the model of the Tennessee Valley Authority, national health insurance, the inevitable price controls, and on and on. He opposed the decontrol of the price of natural gas, a reckless move that would have accelerated the 1973 energy crisis had he not been forced to change his mind to win the support of a key Oklahoma senator. And again his program was largely disregarded.

Then came a great opportunity: another war. Within three months of the North Korean attack on the South, Truman extracted a Defense Production Act from Congress, at last permitting him to re-impose the economic controls he had been demanding for five years. Embittered liberals damned the results of the elections of November 1950—a Democratic loss of five seats in the Senate, and twenty-eight in the House—as a victory for McCarthyism. Perhaps so, but it was Truman's determination to use Korea to reimpose central economic planning that gave McCarthy his opportunity.

Actually, the connection between Truman and McCarthyism is even more direct than that. Senator McCarthy delivered his notorious Wheeling, West Virginia, speech—inaugurating his career as America's premier anticommunist—in January 1950. Previously, most Republican leaders had eschewed McCarthyite demagoguery. Dewey had passionately opposed the outlawing of the Communist party in 1948: "It is an attempt to beat down ideas with a club. It is a surrender of everything we believe in." Two years later, the courtly Robert Taft was prepared to make use of McCarthy; in 1952, Eisenhower—who despised the Wisconsin senator—paid him compliments while campaigning in Milwaukee. What changed their minds?

Perhaps one should ask, who changed their minds? The nostalgic memory of the "Give 'em hell Harry" whistlestop campaign of 1948 has softened our recollection of the extraordinary savagery of Truman's campaign rhetoric. McCullough averts his eyes from the spectacle, inserting only a few rough remarks into his honey-glazed account of Truman's speeches. ("He expressed love of home, love of the land, the virtues and old verities of small-town America, his America. . . . He was friendly, cheerful. And full of fight. 'You are the government,' he said time after time. 'I think the government belongs to you and me as private citizens.' " etc.) Even the more realistic Hamby does not quite convey the full flavor of it.

In Iowa, Truman accused the Republicans of promoting a "Wall Street economic dictatorship." The Congress, he said, "had stuck a pitchfork in the farmer's back."

"That's how they love the farmers!" he roared in Missouri. "They want to bust them just like they did in 1932."

In Detroit, he told a rally that Dewey's election would "totally enslave the workingman." Under a Republican administration, not only would wages fall, "our democratic institutions of free labor and free enterprise" would be endangered.

A Nevada speech condemned the Republicans as "silent and cunning men, who have developed a dangerous lust for power and privilege." In Texas he charged that Republicans opposed government construction of hydroelectric dams "because it means that the big power monopolies cannot get their rake-off at the expense of the public."

In Indiana, the president swung wildly, shouting: "If anybody in this country is friendly to the Communists, it is the Republicans." Again in Oklahoma, Truman tested this proto-McCarthyite theme: "Just why are the Communists backing the third party? [Henry Wallace's Progressives] They are backing the third party because they want a Republican victory in November."

Incessantly, Truman warned that Dewey's election would bring back the Depression. H. L. Mencken, covering his last national campaign, quipped, "If he did not come out for spiritualism, chiropractic, psychotherapy, and extra sensory perception, it was only because no one demanded that he do so. If there had been any formidable body of cannibals in the country, he would have promised to provide them with free missionaries fattened at the taxpayers' expense."

None of Truman's railway-car orations, however, quite matched in viciousness the speech he gave to a huge crowd and nationwide radio audience in Chicago on October 25, vilifying Dewey's campaign themes of national unity and administrative efficiency. Dewey's biographer, Richard Norton Smith, gives this description: "Now he went further, charging that Dewey's party paid only 'lip service' to democracy itself. 'In our time we have seen the tragedy of the Italian and German peoples, who lost their freedom to men who made promises of unity and efficiency and sincerity . . . and it could happen here.' Pointing a finger at 'powerful reactionary forces which are silently undermining our democ-ratic institutions,' Truman accused Dewey of being a 'front man' for the same cliques that had backed Hitler in Germany, Mussolini in Italy, and Tojo in Japan."

Dewey never responded in kind. It's not hard to understand why the Republicans who had lost the 1948 election to a Truman who accused them of fronting for fascism succumbed in 1950 to the temptation to retaliate by representing the Democrats as fronting for communism. What is hard to understand is why McCarthy's lies are regarded as the ultimate in political baseness, while Truman's are laughed off as the amusing excesses of a lovable old cuss.

Since his unlamented departure from office—by which time he had sunk so low in public esteem that the 1952 Democratic presidential nominee, Adlai Stevenson, avoided appearing in public with him—Harry Truman's reputation has been puffed by a series of promoters, all of them in the service of an agenda. First to set the Truman boom in motion was Merle Miller, a journalist who had interviewed Truman at length in the early 1960s, and then reproduced extracts from those interviews in a 1974 book, *Plain Speaking*. In a country weary of the deceit of Lyndon Johnson and Richard Nixon, *Plain Speaking* inspired nostalgia for the days when it had been governed by a simple, direct man who minced no words. (Ironically enough, the best stories in it are completely untrue.)

As the post-Vietnam Democratic party abandoned its commitment to containment, Truman took on talismanic meaning for the dwindling handful of Democrats who kept faith with liberal anti-communism. What better symbol of their politics could the party's history offer than a president who faced down Moscow abroad while veering further left on domestic issues than any important Democrat of the 1970s would dare? For Republicans who wanted to reach out to hawkish Democrats who felt abandoned by their ancestral party, Truman likewise became a potent symbol. And everyone, Democrat or Republican, who retained some elemental faith in the country's conduct of the great struggles of the century felt obliged to vindicate Truman against the revisionists who blamed him for dropping an allegedly unnecessary atomic bomb on an allegedly helpless Japan and forcing confrontation on an allegedly peace-loving Soviet Union.

In the aftermath of the Cold War, however, Truman's legacy has become available for more sinister exploitation by politicians who want to incite the poor against the successful, who want to revitalize discredited schemes of statism, who want the press corps to chuckle indulgently as they violently defame their opponents. No wonder Bill Clinton has become so interested in him.

PART II

Public Policy

You're on Your Own

For two generations, Republicans have fought Big Government the way a starved wolf hunts a herd of deer, hanging back out of harm's way and waiting for an old buck to stumble. Seldom have they troubled to think through a coherent answer to the central problem of welfare-state politics: which social welfare programs should the state support, and which should it not?

In the past, Republican incoherence on the subject of Big Government was usually justified on practical grounds: The voters liked big government, and, as George Bernard Shaw once said, "democracy is the theory that the voters know what they want and deserve to get it good and hard." Prudent Republicans, even if they disliked the welfare state, kept quiet and tried not to sound heartless. Now, though, Republicans face an embarrassing political difficulty—and maybe an opportunity. The angry sound of talk radio; the mass resignation of congressional incumbents before the 1992 election; the Perot vote—all warn that some large portion of the voters is seething with rage against Washington and its ways.

But so far voter alienation has not translated into many Republican victories. Democrats control the White House, the Senate, the House and a majority of the statehouses: Not since the aftermath of Watergate have they enjoyed such unchecked power.

Voter anger, and the apparent inability of conservatives to tap it, is a bitter byproduct of welfarism. The welfare state is a highly rickety contraption. Its costs rise faster than its revenues, because the underlying economy's growth slows under the weight of the welfare state's demand for taxes. Deficits, debts, and crushing interest costs ensue. In the U.S., interest costs now consume 14 percent of federal revenues. Sooner or later, voters sense that they are receiving only eighty-six cents worth of government for every dollar they pay in taxes—actually less, given bureaucratic inefficiencies. They become suspicious and angry.

Parties of the left can cheerfully inflate their way out of this dilemma. Parties of the right, hostile to taxes and inflation but afraid to touch the programs their opponents built, have found it harder to cope. That's one reason that the populist upsurge of the late 1980s and early 1990s has done more damage to conservative than liberal parties, wrecking the popularity of George Bush's administration in the U.S., Conservative governments in Canada and Britain, the Liberal Democrats in Japan, and the Christian Democrats in Italy and probably Germany.

The "end game of the welfare state," as Irving Kristol has called it, may thus present Republicans with no choice but to take a harder line against big government. If they did, what would that hard line look like? Could there be any stopping place short of the ultra-minimal government that some conservatives want but that the American voter has consistently rejected?

A Republican vision of social welfare would have to pass three tests. To satisfy the party's economic conservatives, it must slash at government costs. To satisfy the party's social conservatives, it must eliminate incentives to personal misconduct and family breakup. And to satisfy the party's pragmatists, the vision must be attractive and politically defensible.

One principle that passes all three of those tests goes something like this. Government should protect people only from risks they cannot easily protect themselves against: unemployment, natural disasters, catastrophic illnesses. Government should not protect nonindigent people against the predictable results of their own actions or the inevitable cycles of life—against the costs of retirement and college, against the regular fluctuations of farm and factory prices, against the miseries caused by idleness and addiction.

Such a rule might never be applied with perfect neatness. Government will, for example, always have to do something for the most helpless of the poor: providing school lunches, immunization for children and frugal in-kind aid like food stamps and housing vouchers. But a little inconsistency is OK. Republicans don't apply their opposition to racial preferences neatly either, but voters understand what the Republican position amounts to: individual rights, yes; group rights, no.

As economic conservatives want, a principle of protecting

Americans against only hard-to-predict risks would save a lot of money. Obviously, any changes in the pension system and Medicare would have to be phased in slowly. Representative Chris Cox of California, who sits on Senator Bob Kerrey's entitlements reform commission, has speculated that one way to do that would be to halve the Social Security tax on workers under forty, and let them pay the money into individual retirement accounts instead.

The sums at stake are so colossal that even relatively modest reforms would yield breathtaking results. The Social Security Administration says it does not keep track of the dollar value of the benefits it pays to middle and high-income households. It can say, though, that in 1994 the U.S. will put a total of some $300 billion into pensioner households, about one-fifth of which enjoy incomes of $30,000 or more.

Sickness is almost as predictable as old age, but the second-largest domestic program, Medicare, will spend some $140 billion in 1994 to protect the nonindigent elderly against routine medical problems. At the same time, Medicare fails to protect the elderly against the catastrophic medical expenses for which government help is most needed and most justifiable.

Medicare's elaborate system of deductibles and co-payments was supposed to induce some sense of responsibility in its beneficiaries, but nearly 80 percent of the elderly now purchase private insurance to cover this "gap" or else receive medigap coverage courtesy of Medicaid. Four-fifths of older Americans therefore have sloughed virtually all the costs of health care off their own shoulders—in the process raising their medical expenses, according to one careful estimate, by about 18 percent.

Pensions and Medicare together amount to a $440 billion expenditure. But even the relatively small programs that would get the ax under a predictability test are large enough by non-Washington standards: nearly $13 billion for student loans, a little more than $10 billion for agricultural supply management programs, $11 billion for low-income housing and energy assistance, and $16 billion for Aid to Families with Dependent Children.

A welfare state that protected people only against unforeseeable disasters would not be small. Even so, a predictability test holds out the hope of a one-third or larger reduction in the cost of the federal government's social-welfare programs as the current generation of retirees passes from the scene.

In the past, culturally minded Republicans have rebelled whenever economic conservatives spoke too enthusiastically about practicing a little liposuction on the body politic. They believed that Presidents Nixon and Reagan had created a New Majority, made up of "conservatives of the heart," as Patrick Buchanan calls them. This New Majority was patriotic and religious, but it still hankered after the economic protections invented by Franklin Roosevelt and Harry Truman. For goodness' sake, many Republicans reasoned, why alienate them with radical economics? Stick to Mapplethorpe.

Cutting government benefits that protect people against predictable risks is, however, one economic program that cultural conservatives ought to be able to support. Cultural conservatives bemoan the eclipse of one type of American personality—self-reliant, self-controlled, hardworking and patriotic—and its apparent replacement by another: dependent, hedonistic, narcissistic and whiny.

If cultural conservatives would recognize that the tough old American character they mourn was a rational response to the toughness of American life, they would find their differences with economic conservatives evaporating. Victorian personalities do not flourish in a world of Great Society welfare programs.

Cultural conservatives like William Bennett now recognize that antipoverty programs have stifled self-reliance among the poor. They concede that government-mandated racial preferences have exacerbated inter-group animosity. They should be able to perceive that the Federal Housing Administration and student loans and Social Security bear at least some of the responsibility for corroding the character of the middle class.

Is this political suicide? The welfare state is collapsing about our ears, bankrupting the Treasury, and corrupting the character of the people. Republicans need to say *something* about this unhappy situation. Surely no Republican cost-cutting plan would be easier to explain and defend than a policy of no government help for those who could have taken care of themselves.

Up from Subsidy

Which matters more: friends or principles? This dilemma afflicts all political parties, but seldom does the wrong choice bristle with as much danger as it now does for the new congressional Republican majority.

On principle, of course, the Republicans champion free enterprise and smaller government. But all too many of their friends—agriculture and ranching interests, logging and mining companies, export-oriented manufacturers—have come to expect a helping hand from Uncle Sam. The Cato Institute's Stephen Moore counts 125 federal programs that subsidize business at an annual cost of $85 billion. In his 1995 report "Cut and Invest," Robert Shapiro of the liberal Progressive Policy Institute identified $131 billion in business subsidies that could be cut over the following five years, along with $101 billion in highly targeted tax exemptions.

Such vast sums are big enough to do more than put a bulge in overall federal spending. As Shapiro points out, they also distort the American economy by attracting excessive investment to the most heavily subsidized industries: farming, energy production, and transportation. But the harm done by federal subsidies to business cannot be measured in dollars alone.

The massive repudiation of the Democrats last November should not automatically be interpreted as a declaration of confidence in the Republican Party. Newt Gingrich's victory came only twenty-four months after the party's presidential nominee collected a smaller proportion of the vote than any nominee since Alf Landon in 1936. While the word "conservative" elicits positive feelings in opinion surveys, pollster Frank Luntz reports, the word "Republican" still does not. The steady, high support for term limits—even after voters demonstrated they can toss out-of-touch incumbents out by themselves—suggests a continuing mistrust of the institution of Congress.

Elected officials warn that the voter wrath that immolated Tom Foley and his pals could easily turn against an out-of-touch Republican Party. What was rejected in November, Arizona Senator John McCain has argued, was not merely liberalism as an ideology—it was interest-group politics as a way of doing business. If that's right, *how* the new Republican majority produces laws may be just as important as the actual *content* of those laws. Republicans' willingness to disregard the immediate self-interest of their constituencies may matter as much to voters as the size of their tax cuts or the toughness of their crime bill.

Unfortunately, the Republicans have been sending some ominous signals that business in Washington is continuing as usual. The *Washington Post* reported in March 1995 one petty but obnoxious example: although the Republican welfare reform plan enacted by the House in March abolished federal benefits for immigrants under age seventy-five, it made one exception—for temporary farm laborers. These workers will remain eligible for food stamps, Medicaid, and other benefits likely to lower the employment bills of large food producers. Nobody will say who inserted this provision into the act, but everyone understands how it got there and who profits from it.

Even more startling was the last-minute amendment of the Republicans' "private-property protection act," which defined any federal action to reduce the generosity of the subsidies to users of federal water projects as a compensable "taking" under the Fifth Amendment. The magnitude of this gift is not easy for those in the puny East to comprehend: the lucky farmers and miners who receive water from federal irrigation systems like California's Central Valley Project pay $15 or less per acre-foot (more than 300,000 gallons) of water. The cost of pumping water through the pharaonically uneconomic CVP is an amazing $1,800 per acre-foot or more. The market price for traded water in California oscillates between $250 and $400 per acre-foot. To big beneficiaries, the federal water subsidy can be worth up to $12 million per year.

Perhaps, as defenders of the subsidy argue, it would be injudicious to withdraw it suddenly and without warning. But the recipients of these subsidies have as much of a *moral* claim to compensation as the socialist socialites of Central Park West would if New York City asked them to pay the real value of their rent-controlled nine-room apartments.

These actions do not in themselves condemn the entire Republican Party. The new congressional majority will need decades to catch up to the venality and corruption of the Democrats. Even the far-left *Mother Jones* magazine, in an April 1995 cover story itemizing all the ways that the GOP will blight America, began by conceding that the new Republican majority is far more honest than the defeated and unlamented machine pols who ran the House between 1954 and 1994. But what the farm and water-rights stories do indicate is that, unsupervised, congressional Republicans can succumb to the institutional corruption that felled the Democrats.

Indeed, the list of business subsidies collected by Moore and Shapiro stands as a waxwork chamber of horrors of institutional corruption. Shapiro contends that $2 billion could be saved over the next five years by ceasing to subsidize profitable utility companies in the name of rural electrification, and $3.5 billion more could be picked up by telling energy companies to fund their own research and development.

Congress has been tucking money into the pockets of General Motors, Citibank, and American Airlines; of Florida's wealthiest sugar growers and Georgia's logging barons; and—through neat manipulations of the tax code—of the construction and insurance industries. It has been underwriting the foreign advertising of McDonald's and Sunkist, exempting credit unions from taxes that other savings institutions must pay, and assuming the research expenses of Intel, IBM, and other semiconductor manufacturers.

Putting an end to this nonsense would invigorate the economy by freeing capital to flow to its most productive use, and go far toward balancing the budget—and financing general tax cuts that would do vastly more to invigorate business than any amount of special favors. But striking at industry subsidies would also immensely strengthen the Republicans politically. In three ways:

• By ceremoniously and ostentatiously decapitating hundreds of programs for giant corporations, rich farmers, and multinational enterprises, the Republicans could prove to a skeptical electorate the sincerity of their free-market principles. Voters do not need to agree with principles to respect them. And nothing would underscore the Republican commitment to principle—no matter whose ox is gored—than the sounds of big Dole contributor Dwayne Andreas of Archer Daniels Midland

and other corporate welfare queens squealing in outrage at the loss of their subsidies and tax exemptions.

• Attacking corporate subsidies may also help to insulate Republicans from accusations of callousness as they reform welfare and middle-class entitlements. Purging the budget of special favors for big companies cannot substitute for welfare and entitlement reform—relatively few farmers, after all, are getting pregnant out of wedlock and spraying street corners with machine-gun bullets. But a strong record on the business subsidy issue will give nervous Republican congressmen something to say when the *New York Times* accuses them of starving orphans.

• Finally, there is partisan hay to be made out of the business-subsidy issue. While it was a November speech by Labor secretary Robert Reich, praising the first draft of Robert Shapiro's research, that ignited the current round of debate on "aid to dependent corporations," it remains true that the Clinton administration has enthusiastically showered money on favored corporations. Indeed, it was Robert Reich's own academic work—which enthusiastically champions targeted subsidies and trade protection to "strategic" companies and industries—that provided the administration with its main economic ideas. Should President Clinton blast his Republican rival in 1996 for cozying up to the rich, the GOP candidate might want to tick off some of the items on Moore's list of Clinton handouts:

> —$490 million for the Advanced Technology Project (ATP), the Clinton administration's high-tech version of the Small Business Administration. Last year the administration provided grant funds to such industry giants as General Electric, United Airlines, Xerox, Dupont, and Caterpillar . . .

> —$500 million for the Technology Reinvestment Project, a newly created military defense conversion program that subsidizes the development of civilian technologies. In 1994 award recipients included such Fortune 500 companies as Texas Instruments ($13 million), 3M ($6 million), Chrysler Corporation ($6 million), Hewlett Packard ($10 million), Boeing ($7 million), and Rockwell ($7 million) . . .

> —$333 million for the New Generation of Vehicles program, or the "Clean Car Initiative."

—$9.4 billion in small business loan guarantees—an increase of nearly 50 percent since 1993.

The enthusiasm of a Democratic group like the Progressive Policy Institute for slashing business subsidies may worry some Republicans. And any plan labeled "Cut and Invest" understandably raises Republican hackles. But Republicans can swallow their qualms. The elimination of business subsidies no more belongs to President Clinton than does welfare reform or any of the other ideas that PPI has tossed out over the past six years in a remarkably unsuccessful effort to save the Democratic Party from itself. True, President Clinton made his first major post-election appearance of 1994 at a black-tie dinner sponsored by the PPI, but he came to talk, not to listen. The PPI's proposals for "investment" are located in chapters of their own, clearly identified, so conservative readers can skip over them. As for the rest—Republicans should shamelessly steal it.

A New Supply-Side Strategy

Does the fact that a policy is driven by polling and cynicism in itself prove the policy wrong? If the answer is yes, then nothing could be more wrong than the Contract with America's $500-per-child tax credit. The credit flatly defies conservatism's economic logic. It does not create incentives to work or invest. True, the credit may spur consumer spending by parents—but Republican anti-Keynesians have disparaged the growth-inducing powers of consumer spending for two decades now. No wonder that some economics-minded conservatives can be heard grumbling that they would like to junk the credit—or that it has encountered such skepticism in the Senate.

And in fact, there's much not to like about the credit. Through the 1970s, a Democratic Congress mucked up the tax code with incentives for investment choices the legislators liked: investment in cattle ranches and oil wells, solar energy, and the renovation of historic buildings. This favoritism produced notoriously perverse results. Subsidizing investment in farmland, for example, helped push the price of land to unsustainable heights, exacerbating the collapse of farm values in the early 1980s, which in turn contributed to the doom of the family farms Congress was trying to protect. The tax reform of 1986 finally purged the code of some of these rococo elements, but congressional tax writers still often presume to know better than the market where investment capital should flow.

Now the mood has shifted, and the new Republican Congress wants to use the tax code to encourage correct moral behavior instead of correct investment behavior. The Contract with America promised not merely a per-child tax credit, but a refundable credit of up to $5,000 for families that adopt children and a $500 credit for families that care for an elderly parent or grandparent at home. The conduct to be encouraged by the Contract's credits is, to be sure, genuinely laudable. But it's easy to see the temptations opened up by this new style of tax preference for socially desirable actions: President Clinton has already responded to the Contract by proposing new tax advantages for spending on education. Why not tax credits for employers who employ a certain number of blacks or disabled people? In a country beginning to recognize divorce as a massive problem, what about a tax credit for couples who have remained married for ten years? And a bigger credit on the twenty-fifth anniversary?

Please recall what the tax code is for: not social engineering, but raising revenue for the government in the manner that distorts private decision-making the least. That argues for a simple tax on either income or consumption, at low rates, with the smallest feasible number of exemptions, deductions, and credits.

Unfortunately, the United States does not happen to possess such a textbook tax code, and likely never will. The mortgage interest deduction, for example, is virtually impossible to justify economically, but its existence has been factored into the value of every dwelling unit in the country. Abolishing it now would capsize the housing market. So it remains in the tax code, much the way the old English doctrine that you cannot sue the government without its consent hangs on in tort law—a total illogicality fossilized by the sheer passage of time.

By promoting over-investment in housing at the expense of other things, the mortgage interest deduction has done far more harm than any child credit ever could. And yet economists and business-oriented conservatives generally have made their peace with that exception to tax purity. It's not unreasonable to ask them to extend equivalent charity to a per-child credit.

Why? In order to right a glaring wrong: the remorseless rise in the federal tax obligations of middle-income taxpayers, while other taxpayers enjoyed true tax cuts.

Between 1981 and 1987, Ronald Reagan did indeed relieve the income tax burdens of middle-income people: a family of four earning the median income ($26,000 in 1981) paid 11.79 percent of that income in income taxes on Reagan's Inaugural Day, and just 8.9 percent six years later. As they chanted at the 1988 presidential convention, "Thank you, Ron!"

But mounting payroll tax charges gobbled virtually all of that tax relief up: between 1980 and 1990, the combined employer-employee payroll tax rate rose from 12.26 to 15.3 percent. A shoe salesman reviewing his pay stubs would see a gratifying drop in the box marked "income taxes," but an almost exactly equivalent jump in the box marked "FICA." His take-home pay hardly budged. No wonder polls showed the public responding to Democratic cries for higher taxes on the rich in 1988; no wonder that Bill Clinton's promise of a middle-class tax cut thrust him into first place among Democrats before a single primary vote had been cast in 1992.

President Clinton's breach of that promise now opens a magnificent Republican opportunity. In the early 1980s, at a time of economic stagnation, some supply-siders disparaged the economic significance of the tax burdens on the middle class. In his memoir of the early years of the Reagan administration, former assistant Treasury secretary Paul Craig Roberts sharply distinguished between "lower average tax rates, which do not improve incentives, and lower marginal rates, which do." He was, of course, correct. But improving incentives ought not to exhaust the goals of conservative economic policy. Letting people—including middle-income people—keep more of the money they earn is a value in itself, a value that conservatives above all others ought to cherish; and a value, ahem, that scoops up votes.

Since 1987 the tax plight of middle-income people has sharply worsened. Families at the median income (now $42,000) pay more in federal taxes of all kinds than ever before. Meanwhile, their wealthier compatriots still enjoy tax rates generally lower than those they faced in the early 1980s, while millions of poorer people have been dropped from the rolls altogether by the 1986 tax reform and Bill Clinton's expansion of the fraud-plagued Earned Income Tax Credit. Twice in three years the middle class has begged for help—once by electing Bill Clinton in 1992 and then again by electing a Republican majority in 1994. Twice they have been cheated—by George Bush when he broke his "read my lips" pledge and by Clinton when he reneged on his tax-cut pledge. And each time they have promptly wreaked punishment on the politicians who deceived them. That alone should give pause to any senator pondering shelving the per-child credit.

The achievements of supply-side economics in the 1980s were very real. Tax cuts ignited a stagnant economy, and lower tax rates reaped a fat harvest of revenues for Washington. Collections from the combined personal income tax and corporate income tax soared by nearly 60 percent between 1981 and 1990, despite dramatically lower rates. But the political deficiencies of the supply-side were real, too. Unfortunately, to understand why supply-side lost its glamour, you must hold your nose and immerse yourself in the complexities of the tax code.

Imagine an unmarried taxpayer earning $50,000 a year. He faces a *marginal* federal income tax rate of 28 percent—meaning that if he gets a $1,000 raise, he takes home $720 more. But that doesn't mean he's paying 28 percent of his income in taxes. He pays a federal income tax of only 15 percent on his first $22,100 in income. As a result, his effective average federal income tax rate clocks in at about 20 percent, not counting payroll or state taxes.

The average tax rate and the marginal tax rate need not move in tandem. It's quite possible for marginal rates to plunge without affecting average rates very much at all—and that's pretty close to what happened in the 1980s. Marginal tax rates dropped precipitously (from up to 70 percent in 1980 to a maximum of 28 percent in 1987), while average tax rates drifted downward far less dramatically.

Why? Because so few Americans earn really big incomes, it's possible to cut their marginal rates of tax dramatically without costing the Treasury very much income. More important still, because upper-income people typically have more control over how hard they work and how much income they declare, lowering marginal rates on them can actually raise *more* revenue. But even a modest reduction in the average rate of tax paid by the colossal American middle class can cost Washington dozens of billions of dollars. One of the beauties of a cut in the marginal rate is that it permits reluctant budget-cutters to represent themselves as tax slashers. Cuts in the marginal rate can, under the right circumstances, even be financed by the economic growth they spark. Cuts in the average rate of tax on middle-class families cannot. Middle-class tax cuts— tax cuts that bring down the average rate of tax—must be financed by reductions in government spending. No wonder they give senators the willies.

Nervous Republican senators should understand, however, that rejecting the middle-income tax cut can also have scary consequences. In the Bush administration, Senator Daniel Patrick Moynihan complained, correctly, that the 15.3-percent payroll tax raises vastly more money than the Social Security system disburses. Theoretically, that surplus is being accumulated for disbursement in future years. But of course, it's really being spent—in exchange for IOUs to Social Security from the Treasury. Moynihan proposed cutting back this payroll tax until it raised no more money than was currently needed to pay Social Security benefits. That would have added $50 billion to the deficit—money that Moynihan hoped and expected to recoup by levying heavier income taxes in place of the regressive payroll tax.

The Democrats, with their customary death wish, brushed Moynihan's plan aside. But it's still moldering in their arsenal, ready to be used by liberal politicians clever and more ruthless than the current feckless bunch. The Republicans would be wise to head the Democrats off at this particular pass—and the per-child tax credit is one of the least bad ways to do it.

Compassion for Taxpayers

"A humane budget." That's what Canadian Finance Minister Paul Martin promised as he prepared his Spring 1995 budget. The arrogation of terms such as "humanity" and "compassion" by those who advocate ever-costlier government has been stale for a generation. Now it has begun to stink. How is it humane to punish people for working?

Ponder the plight of a typical young Canadian family. After taxes, inflation and currency depreciation, the husband is probably making less than his father did in 1972. To make ends meet, the wife must work and the baby must go to day care. They cannot begin to save adequately—even though they suspect the government pension plans that so generously reward the current generation of retirees won't be there for them. Almost certainly they will have to postpone retirement two or three years longer than their parents did.

Taxes and regulations have raised the price of housing so high as to shove them into a distant suburb. Because both parents work, the family must operate two cars—and pay twice as much gasoline tax. Worst of all, as things are going, it seems highly unlikely that this young family's situation will ever improve: average after-tax incomes have been falling in Canada for more than half a decade.

How is it "humane" to tax these people more? How is it "humane" to heap new surtaxes on them, to threaten their tax-deferred retirement accounts, to make them pay more for gasoline or telephone calls or the small pleasure of a glass of wine or beer?

How is it "humane" to impose new corporate taxes that sap the vitality of the economy, that suck up profits that might otherwise be distributed to employees in higher wages or plowed into job-creating investment? How is it "humane" to shrug off the slide in the value of the Canadian dollar—a slide that has corroded that family's savings and that frightens away foreign investment? How is it "humane" to tax capital so heavily that people who might otherwise have built businesses in Canada flee the country for England or Bermuda?

Paul Martin might answer that taxes are "humane" because the alternative—spending less—is even worse. For the political fortunes of his Liberal party, no doubt spending less is the worse alternative. But from a moral, rather than a political, point of view, it is far from "humane" to use dollars that working families could make better use of to fund ethnic folk-dancing in downtown Toronto, audience-less film production in Quebec, and vote-buying road-construction in rural Nova Scotia. There's no "humanity" in spending British Columbia's money to pay Newfoundland fishermen not to fish. There's no "compassion" in taxing working women in Calgary so that the embittered feminists of the National Action Committee can fly to conferences to abuse those women's husbands.

Canada does not spend $40 billion a year more than it can afford because Canadians are "humane"—Canada spends more than it can afford because Canadian governments have lacked the courage to say "no" to the greedy regional and ideological interest groups that drive federal spending. What politicians call "humanity" amounts in fact to cowardice in pursuit of political power.

Canada is in desperate straits, caused almost entirely by the unwillingness of its governments, federal and provincial, to live within their means. Governments have struggled to escape those straits by heaping new taxes upon the people, even as government spending continued its unabated rise.

For six months, Paul Martin has been promising that his 1995 budget will be different: that this time, at last, it will be government—and not the citizens—that will be asked to make sacrifices. That promise will be vitiated if the budget contains yet another round of taxes; and it will be a mockery of political morality if those taxes are justified with slogans such as "humanity" and "compassion."

The philosopher Aristotle astutely observed that courage is the first of all virtues because without it, the other virtues are useless. A patriot who lacks courage won't defend his country in war. An honest man who lacks courage can be bullied into lying. And without courage, a compassionate country will have its charity misappropriated by the loud and ruthless.

What is needed from Ottawa is the courage to show some compassion—for once—for an overtaxed middle class, and to defy the demands of pressure groups. Quitting the redistribution business would not only represent the truest form of humanity under the present circumstances; it would represent justice.

Working for the Man

It's amazing: a million and a half able-bodied people are enjoying free housing, free meals, television, libraries, educational services, and gymnasiums all without working and all at the expense of the American taxpayer. All they had to qualify for this deal: kill, rob, or rape somebody.

In a May 1995 address to the National Rifle Association, presidential contender Phil Gramm denounced the absurdity of this government-run hospitality business, and proposed that the federal government should attempt to defray half the cost of the federal prison system by putting prisoners to work. This idea provoked some skeptical harumphing from prison administrators, for in fact prison labor has not recently proven a great success. And when questioned, Gramm's staff admitted that they had undertaken no research at all into the practicability of the senator's commitment.

That was careless of the Gramm campaign. Barely a week before, the *Orange County Register* had printed a searing denunciation of the largest employer of convict labor in America: the California Prison Industry Authority. Despite the endless ingenuity of Congress in inventing new federal offenses, prisons remain a local business. The California prison system is the largest in the nation; that one state alone holds nearly twice as many prisoners as the federal government, and at more than twice the expense. Aided by a monopoly on state purchasing, prison industries are big business in California, with sales of some $135 million in 1993–94.

Unfortunately, in five of the past twelve years, California's prison industries cost the state more money than they brought in—despite their monopoly and despite average wages of fifty-six cents an hour, factory space that's practically free, and no taxes or benefits to pay. And while a $3 million profit was turned in 1993–94, that $3 million forced even bigger hidden costs onto the taxpayer, disguised by the ridiculously high prices paid by the state agencies that must buy from the prison industry monopoly.

Among many examples found by the *Register*: California State Polytechnic University in Pomona wanted 213 chairs to outfit a new computer lab. A private contractor could have provided the chairs within six weeks at a price of $54 each; instead, the university was required to pay $92 per chair to the prison industries authority—and to wait nearly a year. "Prison industries," the *Register* concludes, "has a history of providing shoddy, overpriced products." And, as an added irritant, California was also employing hundreds of nonconvict shop foremen, superintendents and salesmen—and paying them wages well above those earned by comparable employees in the private sector.

None of the other forty-one states that use prison labor has compiled a record as bad as California's. And some have done really quite well: North Carolina earned $5.4 million on sales of $51.2 million in 1994, and Texas has made money from prison industries in every year since it began its modern labor program in 1963. But North Carolina's $5.4 million profit does not make much of a dent in the $360 million the state spends each year on its prisons. And Texas's achievement of putting 8 percent of the state's 94,000 prisoners to work—while impressive compared to California's 5 percent and the even lower percentages elsewhere— still leaves work a marginal activity within the correction system.

Do these sorry results prove the prison administrators right and Senator Gramm wrong? Not according to one of the country's emerging authorities on crime and punishment, Andrew Peyton Thomas, a young assistant attorney general in Arizona and the author of *Crime and the Sacking of America.* Thomas points out that in the late nineteenth century, more than 70 percent of state prisoners worked—usually by a lease system, in which the state hired them out to private employers. It was union-sponsored legislation, not economics, that brought prison labor to an end. In the first years of the twentieth century, many states banned prison labor outright; others followed New York in permitting only state agencies to purchase prison-made goods. In 1929, Congress gave states the authority to forbid private purchases of goods made by prisoners in *other* states. Two pieces of New Deal legislation, in 1936 and 1940, effectively suppressed the sale of prison-made goods to private purchasers altogether. Ever since, state government has been the sole market for the products of prison labor. (Which is perhaps the one flimsy silver lining to the amazing expansion of state government since the 1950s.)

"The original conception of the penitentiary was thus turned on its head," Thomas laments. "Prison labor, once viewed as indispensable for restoring a healthy relationship between the criminal and society, was made literally a federal offense. Instead of ceding certain jobs to prisoners to aid in their reformation . . . Americans sought crime control on the cheap. As it turned out, those jobs were eventually lost anyhow to lower-paid foreigners."

Abolish congressional and state restrictions, Thomas says, and prisons will once again bustle with productive labor—and with the rehabilitation labor brings. "The opportunities for discipline and introspection uniquely offered by labor, especially hard labor, is still lost on many of us. . . . If America's prisoners are given work and discipline and required to confront their transgressions as sins against their neighbors, sins for which they are individually responsible, prisons could actually prove beneficial for a change."

Thomas observes that work contributes powerfully to rehabilitation: only 6.6 percent of the federal prisoners who worked were rearrested or violated parole within a year of release, while 20 percent of other federal prisoners found themselves in trouble with the law again. The experience of the one state work program to keep track of its alumni corroborates Thomas: 18 percent of Florida's working convicts return to prison, compared to 50 percent of the nonworking majority.

Of course, it's possible that the cause-and-effect runs the other way round: that the prisoners most eager to mend their ways are the ones who sign up for work. And it's also possible, as one high-ranking California corrections official fears, that the work most conducive to individual rehabilitation (he cites gardening) is the least remunerative for the state.

Worse, it may be true that as the proportion of prisoners enrolled in work programs rises, the value of prison labor's output may tumble. If the 5 percent of California's prisoners who choose to work now need eight times as long as a private manufacturer to build a chair and charge twice as much, what kind of job can we expect from the other 95 percent? Even at fifty cents an hour, prison labor may prove no bargain compared to eager hands equipped with the latest productivity-enhancing tools.

All the same, the experiment is worth a try, and the federal system is probably the best place to start. The people in the federal prisons usually landed there because they committed a crime that required a little more intelligence than the squalid robberies and wife-killings that fill the state prisons: crimes like drug smuggling, counterfeiting and kidnaping. Motivate them with money and perks like better food, and they may go some long way toward reimbursing the taxpayer the $800 million paid for their incarceration.

And if putting prisoners—not just a tiny minority, but virtually all prisoners—to work makes economic sense federally, think what it could do for the states, where prison costs more than $10.5 billion annually and hundreds of millions more for county and municipal jails.

What to Do About
Health Care

In the 1970s, an East German defector to the West was assigned the task of helping other escapees adjust to life in a free country. The problem, he remembered years later, was that from kindergarten through college, from the moment the newspaper was opened in the morning to the moment the radio was turned off at night, every East German was bombarded by state propaganda telling him that the West was afflicted by hideous poverty, unemployment, and crime. As a result, East Germans naturally concluded that in the West poverty, unemployment, and crime were completely unknown.

In the same way, after two years of hearing President Clinton insist that health care was the gravest problem the country faced, it was natural for the President's political opponents to conclude that health care is one subject they need never think about again. A consensus has rapidly formed that Clinton's health-care campaign blighted his presidency. Americans are by and large content with the care they get. They mistrust federal plans to tinker with that care. And other social problems—crime, welfare, immigration—worry them far more. Would it not be wiser to leave the vexed thing alone?

Unfortunately, the mere fact that President Clinton identified health care as an urgent national problem does not automatically prove that it is *not* an urgent national problem. It is, and will remain so.

The persistence and intractability of the health-care problem should not rehabilitate the President's plan. Looking again at this plan, and at the torrent of papers and articles that explicated and

119

defended it, one can only gape at its arrogance and unreality. Apologists insist that it was by no means the socialist document it was represented to be, that it included a dose of market competition. Perhaps so; but this dose of competition was, in a curious sense, the ultimate hubris: the plan's chief architects, Ira Magaziner and Hillary Rodham Clinton, regarded markets not as an infinite series of voluntary exchanges, but as a mechanism, as one more device for state control. They flattered themselves that they could introduce market-like arrangements where they pleased, bar them where they liked, and generally manipulate them to produce desired results.

Even that, however, does not quite convey the full ambition of the plan Magaziner and Mrs. Clinton wrote for the President. The Clinton plan in the minds of its authors aimed at nothing less than slyly reviving the dying hopes of liberalism. Thus: health care would displace busing as a means of compelling racial integration, since the plan's compulsory-insurance cachements would group cities and their inner and outer suburbs together. Health care would be the method for snuffing out the independence of university medical and science faculties, as state and federal officials determined which specialties would be taught, to how many students, and from which ethnic backgrounds. Health care would enable Washington to deliver colossal subsidies to favored business interests, by relieving unionized manufacturers of foolishly extended commitments and by offering smaller businesses below-market insurance at rates to be determined by the effectiveness of their lobbying. And health care would revive the Democratic party by proving to an increasingly skeptical middle class that Big Government could once again pay off for them.

Altogether, the Clinton health plan would have amounted to the most ambitious peacetime assertion of state power over civil society since the National Recovery Act of 1935. Its collapse must be reckoned as one of the closest shaves in the history of American democracy.

Good luck cannot, however, always be counted on. If Americans are to ward off future versions of the Clinton plan, or worse, believers in a free economy and free institutions must grapple with the same problem that Ira Magaziner and Mrs. Clinton did. Or, actually, the same five problems.

Health care is, in the first place, a *budgetary* problem. Together, Medicare (which goes to retirees regardless of income) and Medicaid (which goes only to the indigent) cost $55 billion when Ronald Reagan took office. Today they cost nearly five times as much. If the growth of these two programs could somehow have been held to the rate of inflation over the past decade-and-a-half, the federal budget would be sitting comfortably in surplus today. Unless these two programs—and other health-care-driven programs like veterans' benefits and federal employees' retirement benefits—can somehow be brought under control in the future, it is impossible to imagine how the federal budget can be balanced and taxes cut.

Second, health care is an *economic* problem. Americans pay more than 13 percent of the national income for health care—more than any other major industrial nation. And the bills keep mounting at an unbelievable clip. One survey of large employers found that their health costs per employee more than doubled in the ten years 1984–93, from $1,645 to $3,781. Small employers' costs have mushroomed even more dramatically. True, prices came off the boil slightly in the mid-1990s—but they are still rising faster than inflation and faster than overall economic growth. The exploding costs of benefits are gobbling up money that might otherwise have been paid to employees in cash: one important reason for wage stagnation during the 1980s boom.

Health care is also a *social* problem. The United States is aging rapidly. While the total population is expected to increase by about 20 percent between 1990 and 2030, the number of Americans older than sixty-five is expected to double. When Americans reach age sixty-five, they enter a new country—one characterized by stark dependence on government. The tilting of the demographic balance toward the old therefore threatens to tilt the country's social balance away from self-reliance and toward welfarism. And even before they reach retirement, many Americans do indeed suffer the anxieties that Mrs. Clinton so passionately described during the debate over her plan: anxieties about losing their insurance if they lose or change their job, and about insurers or employers arbitrarily changing the rules of the plans they rely on.

Inevitably, then, health care will again rise as a *political* problem. One thing, at least, Republicans should have learned from the Bush years—it is not prudent to tell voters who believe they have a problem that they are mistaken. To be sure, most people like the care they get. A major survey done in 1993 on behalf of Novalis Corporation—a consultant to the managed-care industry—found that nearly 80 percent of Americans rated their own personal care as "good" or "excellent." Only 5.4 percent rated the care they were receiving as "poor." Startlingly, more than half of the *un*insured rated *their* care as good or excellent. Even more startlingly, 55 percent of the uninsured reported that they enjoyed the services of a family doctor.

How can this be? For one thing, the typical uninsured American is not the widow Jones and her four hungry children: the Joneses are on Medicaid. The typical uninsured American is a high-school graduate looking for his first job or a recently divorced woman waiting on tables while she tries to put her life back together. Sixty percent of the uninsured are younger than thirty. Most of them will go without insurance for only a short time, just as they will go without employment for a short time: at any given moment, as many as thirty-nine million Americans may lack insurance, but only 4 percent of the population are without it for as long as twenty-eight months.

Since the uninsured are younger and healthier than average, and since state regulators have heaped so many minimum requirements onto private health-insurance plans, conventional policies represent a bad deal for most of these young people. If they could buy a bare-bones policy for $800 or $1,000, many of them might do it. But if forced to buy an expensive plan, they will wait until an employer purchases it on their behalf (not considering that he will submerge the cost by lowering wages).

Yet while Americans like the care they get, they feel no such enthusiasm for the national system as a whole. Only 45 percent rate the health-care system "overall" as excellent or good. Enough bad news has percolated through the population to persuade a majority to rate the *nation's* health care, as against their own personal situation, as fair or poor. Which means that the malfunctioning of the system—its out-of-control costs, and the sense of powerlessness it inflicts on millions of consumers—will again sound a political echo.

Fifth, health care represents a *moral* problem for American democracy. Everywhere one looks, the distorted health-care market has created incentives for squalid behavior. Because Medicaid reimburses hospitals at absurdly low rates, hospitals make up the shortfall by deliberately inflating the bills of their privately insured patients. Because Medicaid covers nursing-home care and Medicare does not, and because Congress in 1988 enacted legislation that prevents Medicaid from investigating the assets of next-of-kin, old people can pass their assets intact to their children and then get cared for by the taxpayer. (This practice has become so routine that Senator Carol Moseley-Braun of Illinois won her race in 1992 despite the revelation that she had engaged in just such asset-shifting in order to qualify her mother for Medicaid.) Because the cost of insurance is escalating so rapidly, even conscientious employers are pressured to scale back the coverage they offer. And because welfare recipients are entitled to Medicaid, but intact low-income working families generally are not, the failures of the American health-care market add one more temptation to the allurements of the dole.

These are big problems, they are urgent problems, and they are difficult problems. But anyone who wants to fix them has to begin by liberating his mind from the illusion the Clinton administration propagated about the American health-care system—the illusion that it is a free-market, private-sector system, and that its faults derive from the brutal appetite for profit.

In fact, health care is among the sectors of the American economy where government's power weighs most heavily. The vast sums of Medicare and Medicaid money pumped into the health market since 1965 helped to spark the medical-cost inflation of the past thirty years. State regulation effectively outlaws cheap health-insurance plans by specifying a long list of services, from acupuncture to psychiatry, that any employer who decides to set up a plan must provide. But the most important of all the government-created distortions of the health market is the way health benefits are taxed.

Suppose you are given a $100-a-week raise by your employer. If you are a professional or managerial worker, you will be lucky to take home $55 of it after income and payroll taxes. If, however, that same $100 were spent to beef up your health insurance, every dollar of it would be available to you. For anyone whose health is not absolutely perfect, $100 of health insurance is more valuable than $100 in cash.

This distortion has twisted health insurance into strange shapes. Compare health insurance to automobile insurance. When you buy a policy, you pay a price calibrated to the riskiness of the car you drive and your own safety history. Automobile insurance is *insurance*—protection against big losses for which you pay a premium determined by the probability that you will incur such a loss.

The policy does not cover new tires, tune-ups, or gasoline.

By contrast, health-insurance premiums are not much influenced by the riskiness of the actual people covered, nor does health insurance pay only against substantial losses. What are conventionally thought of as "good" plans cover eyeglasses, prescription drugs, check-ups, and other routine expenses. In other words, health insurance, for most Americans, is not insurance but a disguised form of salary. It is as if the federal government were to decide that money spent by employers to feed lunch to their employees could be deducted from taxes. And it is as if, instead of paying their employees and sending them out to get their own lunch with after-tax dollars, employers would set up lunchrooms and add asparagus and artichokes to the salad bar whenever profits improved.

Making health insurance a perk rather than insurance causes people to divert more of their income toward health care than they would otherwise prefer. If instead of giving me a raise, my employer juices up my health plan so that I can buy a new pair of eyeglasses every year, new eyeglasses are what I will take—even though I would rather have new shoes for the children or books or a little extra money for groceries.

Noninsurance health insurance also teaches people not to care about the price of the medical services they buy. In their remarkable book, *Patient Power*, John Goodman and Gerald Musgrave asked seven different Dallas-area hospitals the price of a complete blood count. The charge varied from $11 to $33. They found the same disparities for big-ticket services too: the normal delivery of a child could cost anywhere from $1,000 to more than $2,000. The same consumers who would drive across town to save a dollar and a half on a movie ticket neither know nor care what they pay for medical services, because the money they save belongs to their employer, not to them.

Worse, the value of the health-care perk varies not according to your health-care needs, but according to your income. If you are paying a 50-percent marginal tax rate, you would have to earn an extra $6,000 to buy a $3,000 health-insurance policy with after-tax dollars. If you are paying a 25-percent marginal tax rate, you would only need to earn an extra $4,000. Stuart Butler of the Heritage Foundation notes that the nontaxability of health-care fringe benefits amounted to a $48 billion tax expenditure in 1991, most of which was lavished upon the highest-income taxpayers.

Finally, so long as health insurance is thought of as a perk, it will remain a deal not between the consumer and the provider of health services, but between the provider and the consumer's employer. Everywhere else in American society, the past fifteen years have humbled giant bureaucracies. Automakers, the phone company, television networks—every corporation that used to present customers with "take-it-or-leave-it" deals has felt the new power of consumers who enjoy more information and more choices than ever before. But not medicine. There, consumers still approach bureaucracies as dependents and supplicants. Why? Because they typically do not control the money they are spending.

Whatever the Clinton plan's other evils, it was not illogical. Clinton proposed to eliminate the health market's inconsistencies by proceeding faster in the direction the country had been heading since 1965: toward fully state-controlled medicine. Unless his opponents can reverse course and pull the country back toward a free market in health care, something like the Clinton plan must someday prevail. The choice for America does not lie between the Clinton plan and the status quo. The status quo cannot be sustained. The real choice is between some variant of the Clinton plan and free-market reform.

So far, conservatives have produced three main approaches to health-care reform. In 1983, the Reagan administration sought to cap the increase in Medicare costs by stipulating in advance the amount it would pay to hospitals for 467 distinct procedures. Until then, hospitals had set their own prices more or less as they pleased, and mailed the bills to Washington. The Reagan caps did jolt the hospitals and did produce one-time savings. But as hospitals learned the system, the upward march of prices swiftly resumed.

Worse, while the Reagan caps failed to rein in Medicare, they succeeded in lowering the program's standards of care, by setting reimbursement rates for many simple operations below the hospitals' own costs without creating incentives for hospitals to restructure those costs. As a result, Medicare patients often fail to find hospitals willing to perform simple but important services.

The second conservative approach was the individual-mandate plan designed by Heritage's Butler in 1991. Heritage figured that since everyone in the country was getting some form of health coverage anyway, everyone ought to buy it. But unlike most liberal schemes, the Heritage plan imposed the obligation to buy insurance, but on individuals rather than employers.

In order to make insurance affordable to poorer people, the Heritage plan would have had Washington seize the $48-billion tax subsidy to the private-insurance market and redistribute it. If your employer paid $3,000 a year to buy you health insurance, that $3,000 would now count as "income" on your W-2. What you would get instead would be a tax credit for the purchase of health insurance, ranging from 20 percent if you earned a high income to as much as 90 percent if you were very poor.

Thus, an affluent person who bought a $3,000 policy (and he would probably be buying it for himself since the government would no longer be giving his employer a tax subsidy to buy the policy for him) would be able to subtract $600 from his income tax. The remaining $2,400 he would have to pay out of his own pocket with after-tax dollars. That would make him a much more careful shopper. Meanwhile, a low-income person who spent $1,000 on a cheap policy would get a tax credit for as much as $900—and if that $900 exceeded the insured person's income-tax liability, he would get a check for the balance from the IRS.

The Heritage plan would make insurance much more accessible while also inducing Americans to be a little more price-conscious. Upper-income Americans would care about price because they would be paying 80 percent of the cost of their insurance policies themselves with after-tax dollars. Lower-income Americans would care about price because—even though their out-of-pocket costs would nearly vanish—they would be obliged to shop for insurance policies on their own, rather than simply presenting themselves to a doctor who would bill Medicare or Medicaid.

Back in 1992 and early '93, when some type of socialized medicine hovered ominously close, the Heritage plan looked like a daring free-market reform. As backing for the Clinton plan crumbled, though, the redistributionist features of the Heritage scheme cost it most of its support among Republicans. Libertarian-minded Republicans disliked ordering people to buy insurance, and conservatives generally gagged as they realized that Heritage's system of credits would steepen the progressivity of an already redistributionist tax system—an especially sore point after President Clinton hiked the top federal-tax rate to nearly 40 percent (up from 28 percent just five years ago).

Because Medicaid and Medicare would continue to absorb virtually all the health-care costs of the poorest and oldest—in fact, these programs would take on even larger responsibilities—it is doubtful that the Heritage plan would do very much to reduce health care's drain on the federal treasury. Nor would the Heritage plan affect the way Americans react to health costs. From the point of view of the consumer, not much would change: he would go on sending his medical bills to CIGNA or Aetna for reimbursement as he incurred them. All he would notice was that he was paying higher income taxes.

After months of intra-conservative pummeling, Butler surrendered his sword. He co-authored an article in the winter 1995 issue of *Policy Review*, Heritage's quarterly publication, with one of his severest critics, William Niskanen, retreating from the specifics of the 1991 plan to more general principles that nearly all free-market-minded people would accept.

Niskanen is president of the libertarian Cato Institute, and the principles he and Butler promulgated seem to point more naturally to the medical-savings (or Medisave) plan devised by Goodman and Musgrave. All the technicalities aside, Medisave would work more or less like this:

The tax exemption for contributions by employers to health-insurance plans would be abolished in favor of tax-exempt Medisave accounts. Employees and their employers would make donations to these accounts, out of which individuals would pay for their routine medical expenses. Whatever was left over in the account at year's end would remain the saver's property. Over a number of years, reasonably healthy people would compound tidy nest eggs with which to finance their health costs in old age. In the meantime, they would protect themselves against serious illnesses by purchasing a new type of policy, one made available by the repeal of state and federal regulations controlling what a health-insurance policy must look like.

The new policies would carry very high deductibles—as much as $3,000 a year. Since more than 80 percent of Americans spend less than $3,000 a year on health insurance, the premiums for these policies would be relatively low. Large savings could also be made in administrative expenses. As economists often point out, a $50 claim costs as much to process as a $50,000 claim. Under Medisave the vast bulk of medical costs would be paid without having to crank up the bureaucratic machinery of the insurance companies.

Over time, these Medisave accounts would eliminate the need for Medicare. As for Medicaid, it could be replaced either by a more modest version of the Heritage Foundation's tax-credit scheme or else by direct payments by the government to Medisave accounts established for low income people.

The tremendous advantage of the Goodman and Musgrave plan is that it would bring medical cost inflation screeching to a halt. As people bought medical services for themselves, with real dollars that they could otherwise keep, they would suddenly start to shop as cannily for health care as they do for food and shelter and every other essential of life.

And the Goodman and Musgrave scheme would accomplish this while protecting the quality of health care: patients would no longer be subject to an insurer's determination—or Medicare's—of what they did or did not need. They could decide for themselves whether or not they required a third day in the hospital after giving birth; they could decide for themselves whether or not they wanted to pay for a policy that covered psychological trauma.

The weakness of the Goodman and Musgrave plan is that it pays comparatively little attention to the problem of insuring America's poorest. Their Cato allies have suggested that the best answer to this problem lies in forming pools of high-risk people that each state would pay private insurers to take care of. Twenty-eight states have already enacted something very like what Cato recommends. But this remains an inadequate response to the ever-mounting medical ills of America's growing ranks of underclass poor.

What, then, to do? The four main goals of health-care reform are:

- To alleviate the burden that spiraling health costs impose on the federal budget.
- To alleviate the burden that spiraling health costs impose on private industry.
- To bring insurance within easier reach of the uninsured.
- To nip in the bud the deterioration in medical quality that has begun to manifest itself as employers and governments control costs with top-down administrative measures instead of competition.

The Goodman and Musgrave Medisave plan goes far toward accomplishing these goals. It ought to be the basic building block of any Republican reform. But it does not reach quite far enough. Four additional steps are needed.

First, Medicaid—the most rapidly growing and most abused federal-health program—should be reconceived. Instead of being a piece of the health-care puzzle, Medicaid, along with the federal disability program, must be recognized as a piece of the welfare puzzle. Medicaid is already administered by the states, under widely varying rules. Indeed, one man—former New York Governor Mario Cuomo—is almost single-handedly responsible for the explosion of Medicaid costs. New York State, though it contains only 9 percent of the Medicaid population, gobbles up 18 percent of Medicaid spending. Congress should do with Medicaid what it is preparing to do with welfare: cap benefits at their present level, convert the money into block grants to the states, and repeal all rules inhibiting state freedom to experiment.

After all, the tragedies counted among America's most horrific health problems—from premature underweight babies to AIDS-infected drug addicts to the twelve-year-old gunshot victims bleeding to death in lackadaisical ambulances—are not really health problems, any more than the plight of the homeless is a housing problem. They are incidents and by-products of the breakdown of social order among the urban underclass.

Thus, for example, the demographer Nicholas Eberstadt has demonstrated that even though ultra-low-birth-weight babies enjoy better odds of survival in America than in any other country, America still suffers a horrific infant-mortality rate because American mothers give birth to so many more low-weight babies than mothers in other countries. Eberstadt has shown that the most important factor in determining birth weight is the mother's own conduct. Mothers who drink, smoke, eat badly, and take drugs during pregnancy will have low-birth-weight babies—and such mothers are highly likely to be unmarried. So long as the welfare system encourages illegitimacy, Medicaid could double its prenatal spending every single year and still fail to make a dent in America's infant-mortality statistics.

Next, Washington must get out of the business of providing health care itself. The Veterans Administration is the single largest hospital system in the nation—and also a notoriously inefficient and shoddy one. Hospitals are located where long-forgotten Congressmen could profit politically from them. Costs are high, service quality is low. Everybody agrees that veterans have special claims on the public, combat veterans most of all. But those claims could be met, better and more cheaply, if Washington made extra contributions to veterans' Medisave accounts so that they could buy an insurance policy of their choosing. And then the VA's network of inefficient hospitals could be taken off the nation's books.

As Washington turns Medicaid over to the states and veterans' assistance over to the private sector, the states must likewise limit their own ambitions and abandon their habit of interfering in their medical markets. If an insurance company wants to offer a cheap plan that does not cover acupuncture, chiropractic, or replacement eyeglasses, it should be allowed to do so. If a health maintenance organization wants to contract only with a specified list of doctors who agree to follow certain rules, it should be allowed to do that, too—without the state legislature forcing it to deal with "any willing provider." The thirty-nine million uninsured have money to spend. If permitted, the insurance companies will offer policies such people can afford. America has thirty-nine million uninsured people for the same reason that it would have thirty-nine million naked people if the only clothing stores permitted to operate were Bendel's and Saks. We should legalize K-mart insurance before concluding that the private sector cannot do the job.

Finally, America's most permanent and intractable health problem arises from the most permanent and intractable fact of life: old age. It is expensive to be old even if you are comparatively healthy, and it is very expensive if you are not healthy. Beginning in May 2011, the front wedge of the baby boom will turn sixty-five. They are going to need hearing aids and prescription drugs and pacemakers and hip replacements and all the other wonderful contrivances of modern medical technology. And soon afterward, these baby-boomer retirees will need nurses and in-home care and, in the end, institutional care.

All that will require money—huge amounts of money. Whose? As things are going, the money will have to come from a penurious government squeezing all it can out of the baby-bust generation. This effectively guarantees that the baby boomers will receive low-grade care in their declining years. If, however, the money paying those nurses and buying the pacemakers is the retirees' own, they will enjoy an abundance of choices and eager service in health care, as consumers do in every other sector of a market economy.

In order to ensure that they have the money to spend, though, the baby boomers must begin at once to save like chipmunks anticipating a hard winter. Doing that over the hurdles of a 39-percent top federal income-tax rate and a 28-percent capital-gains rate will be no easy trick.

Like everything else, then, the health-care problem turns out to be a corollary of the problem of the growth rate of the U.S. economy and the accumulation of private capital. Four years ago, the Heritage Foundation convened a conference to discuss whether tax reform was the key to health-care reform. It is, but not in the sense Heritage meant. Low taxes, and especially low taxes on saving, are the key to the health reform that matters most: enabling Americans to sock away the money they will require to buy care when they can no longer care for themselves.

As complicated as the American health-care story is, it can be summed up simply. Through its tax policies, and then through the invention of Medicare and Medicaid, the federal government has twisted the health-care market in ways that threaten the government's own solvency and the profitability of every employer in the nation.

Measured in dollars, health care may present the most gargantuan example of unintended consequences in the whole sorry history of modern welfarism. Probably the harm done can never be fully undone. Still, it is possible to lay down the basic principles of a saner future for American health care: put control over health insurance into the hands of the insured, not their employers, and make the costs of insurance visible; get government at all levels out of the business of providing health care for the nonpoor, and get the federal government out of the business of providing health care for the poor.

If the American health-care system remains in its present form, it will, within fifteen more years, bring into existence an enormous voting bloc of retirees utterly dependent on the state for comfort and care in their old age. There is virtually no chance that the era of conservative government promised by the 1994 elections can ensue under those conditions. Hence the health-care argument is more than a technical one, more than an argument about regulations and spending and taxes. If the free-marketeers lose this argument, Medicare and Medicaid will ineluctably bring about a whinier, more dependent culture. If, on the other hand, the free-marketeers win, individual medical-savings accounts will not only make for a better health-care system but will also reinforce the self-reliance, thrift, and self-confidence of the American people.

Building Blocks

Fix it in Washington or in the states? All at once or bit by bit? That's the choice Republicans are facing as they prepare to reform welfare. And the longer you think about it, the tougher the choice looks.

The House Republicans' Contract with America pledged to adopt new federal rules to prohibit cash welfare for mothers under age eighteen; to stop the practice of raising payments for each additional child; to cut total welfare spending; and to impose on recipients a two-years-and-out time limit. Washington would enact these rules, and the states—which administer much of the welfare system, including Medicaid and Aid to Families with Dependent Children—would have to comply.

But at the very moment that this pledge was helping Republicans to win power, many conservatives were rethinking it. Charles Murray published a powerful essay in the December 1994 *Commentary* urging welfare reformers to write off Washington and worry instead about freeing the states to experiment, in the hope that one or more might go so far as to abolish welfare altogether. In practice, this would mean replacing the existing patchwork of federal, state, and federally funded, state-administered programs with big "block grants"—chunks of money the states could use to fight poverty as seemed best to them, subject to only the most general directions from the capital.

The difference between these two approaches—fix it from Washington or decentralize—is more than of merely theoretical interest. Inability to choose between them caused the Republican leadership in the House of Representatives to execute an embarrassing double flip-flop over the food-stamp program in late February. Rightly horrified by the rapid increase in food-stamp costs over the past five years—in post-recession 1994, 27.5 million people received food stamps, up from twenty million in pre-recession 1990—the Republicans at first opted for the decentralizing solution: lump all federal nutrition programs together and load them onto the states. Farm-state Republicans mutinied against this plan, ostensibly because they worried that a state-run food-stamp program would be even more vulnerable to fraud than the leaky federal one. In fact, the farm-state Republicans revolted because food stamps help maintain demand for their constituents' products. Pat Roberts of Kansas, chairman of the House Agriculture Committee, told the *New York Times* that he regarded food stamps as "the ultimate social safety net." And so in a sense they are, for they offer protection to over-leveraged Kansas wheat farmers as well as to the destitute of Chicago and Los Angeles.

Thanks to Roberts and his allies, food stamps managed to scramble back aboard the federal wagon from February 24 to February 28, 1995. Roberts went even further still: not only would Washington administer the program, but food stamps would remain an entitlement, with benefits paid to anyone meeting the eligibility criteria—and no limit on total costs. It took four days for two reform-minded Republican governors, John Engler of Michigan and William Weld of Massachusetts, cajole Speaker Gingrich into taking the matter up. In the end, thanks to Gingrich, the House voted to deliver full responsibility for nutritional programs to the states after all, subject to conditions designed to restrain fraud.

The food-stamp imbroglio foreshadows the bigger choices Republicans and conservatives will face in the welfare reform debate. Columnist Charles Krauthammer has written, for example, that Republicans won control of the Congress by promising to reform welfare, and are therefore honor-bound to fulfill that commitment themselves. Fobbing the task off on the states would amount to a dereliction of duty. William Kristol of the Project for the Republican Future, while hesitantly favoring block grants, recalls the dismal experience of President Nixon's revenue-sharing in the 1970s, and warns against repeating those errors now. States spend money sent them from Washington with far less care than the money they raise from their own taxpayers. The arrival of billions of federal dollars is more likely to relieve the states of fiscal pressure to reform welfare and Medicaid than to spur dramatic action, especially since, as liberal welfare critic Mickey Kaus has written, the prevailing image of governors as reform crusaders is utterly mistaken.

On the other hand, Pat Roberts' Four Days in February should remind us that even a Republican-dominated Congress will almost certainly fail to write an adequate welfare reform bill. By the time Congress finishes with its compromises and concessions, the reform that emerges will not amount to very much. Interviewed in March 1995, Charles Murray said he remained certain that the only route to substantial reform lay through the state capitals. "With welfare," Murray said, "the only way to get major reform is if one state demonstrates a very large effect and also demonstrates that you won't have kids starving in the streets"—by, for example, eliminating all its existing welfare programs and devoting the money instead to adoption services.

So who is right?

Despite the effective arguments of the block-grant critics, the nod has to go to the decentralizers. It should be clear by now that Murray correctly estimated the possibilities for real reform in the House. Now just imagine what the far more conventional Senate will do.

As for the infirmities of state governments, remember that block grants, unlike Nixon-era revenue sharing, are not exactly free money. These grants will come attached to substantial new responsibilities for the states. And they will quickly prove far more fiscally constricting than most observers yet appreciate.

Welfare programs are now designed for limitless growth. Medicaid is perhaps the single most shocking example—up from $20 billion a decade ago to nearly $100 billion this year—but other programs, like Supplemental Security Income, are mushrooming as fast or faster. For Washington to control these costs, it would have to rewrite the rules governing the programs—a complicated, politically fraught, and time-consuming business for a Republican majority with much else on its agenda.

Devolution offers Republicans the chance to say, "That's it! The national contribution to the relief of poverty is"—pick a number—"and not a dime more. It will be that same amount next year, or quite possibly less, but it will be a number set as the result of democratic choice, and not by some out-of-control budget mechanism." What would that mean in practice? Picture a dog on a long chain that spots a cat across the road. It jumps upright and sprints at top speed across the lawn—until the chain snaps it backward.

Or, if you want numbers, look northward at the Canadian experience. Virtually all of Canada's social programs are administered by the provinces; Ottawa traditionally absorbed roughly half the costs. When the debt-plagued federal government decides to scale back, as it periodically does, all it need do is cut along the dotted line—one reason that the Canadian federal budget unveiled on February 27, 1995, could deliver actual dollar decreases in spending on programs: 119 billion Canadian dollars were spent in the 1994–95 fiscal year; 112 billion Canadian dollars are budgeted for 1995–96.

The present division of welfare responsibilities between Washington and the states tempts local governments into reckless choices. Mario Cuomo's New York spent twice as much per patient on Medicaid as California, largely because the governor convinced a large chunk of his voters that the bill was being paid by Washington—as indeed nearly half of it was.

There are only two ways out of this fix: either Washington must assert dramatically *more* authority over local decision-making, which few Republicans would favor, or else it must assert much less. States might abuse their new freedom by stubbornly refusing to reform, but that would be their taxpayers' problem. With the status quo costing more and more, and Washington contributing (as it surely will) less and less, even the most troglodyte states will eventually succumb to reform.

Errors of Commission

So much for blue-ribbon commissions. For a decade, politicians afraid to make tough decisions on the budget have nervously suggested passing their job to panels of bankers and college presidents. *We*, the pols say, are crippled by the sniffishness of the voters, but *they* are free from politics and can ignore the public's squawks and pursue the common good.

In no area of public policy has the call for commissions sounded as loudly and insistently as with the budget. What Washington wants to do to balance the budget—cut Social Security, raise taxes, and protect antipoverty programs—conflicts radically with what the voters want done—protect Social Security, cut taxes, and gut antipoverty programs. But guess what? The bankers and college presidents turn out to scare just as easily as the politicians do. Which is why America's grandest experiment yet with a blue-ribbon budget commission, the Kerrey Commission on entitlements, reported spectacular failure.

In 1993, Senator Bob Kerrey of Nebraska demanded a commission to recommend ways of controlling entitlement spending as his price for supporting President Clinton's first budget. He got his wish in February 1994. He and Senator John Danforth of Missouri were named to chair a thirty-member commission as festooned with blue ribbons as the prize pigs at a country fair: ten senators, ten congressmen, three bankers, a union leader, the president of the United Negro College Fund, etc. The commission handed in its report on January 27, 1995, and the results are ignominious: the commission members couldn't agree on *anything*. They couldn't even agree that the problem they were supposed to investigate—out-of-control spending on entitlement programs—actually exists.

Meanwhile, in the same week that the Kerrey commission's

confession of failure landed on the president's desk, congressional Republicans were beginning to assemble what could turn out to be a comprehensive reform of the $140-billion-per-year Medicare program. Old-fashioned party politics has seldom looked better.

Why couldn't the commissioners agree? Well, why should they have agreed? The hundreds of programs we call "entitlements" together make up the radioactive core of the American welfare state. They include not only giant social insurance programs like Social Security, Medicare, and Medicaid, but also the agriculture budget, veterans' compensation, food stamps and welfare, black-lung payments to coal miners, nutrition aid, and on and on and on. Basically, an entitlement is any program for which Congress, instead of appropriating a fixed sum of money (as it does for defense or transportation), sets up criteria of eligibility and says: anyone who meets these criteria is entitled to government help.

By that definition, roughly half the budget goes to entitlements of one type or another. The hope that you could lock bank presidents, union leaders, and Democratic and Republican politicians in a room together, as the Kerrey commission did, and have them work out some grand deal was a delusion from the start. Not just a delusion but a puzzling delusion: why *should* entitlement reformers put their ideologies aside? Why *aren't* Republicans and Democrats permitted to disagree about whether spending cuts or tax increases should be used to balance Washington's books?

The final report of the entitlements commission confirms how ideological an exercise spending reform necessarily is. Because the commission could not agree on a single set of recommendations, the two chairmen, many of the commissioners, and the commission staff gathered their own various personal plans together into the final report. As a result, the document is sprinkled with literally hundreds of ideas for cutting spending and raising revenues. Commissioner Pete Peterson, for example, proposed a mass of tax increases (principally a huge rollback in the home mortgage deduction) and cuts in benefits to middle-income people. It's an intelligent and comprehensive plan—if you agree that preserving a generous welfare state for the least well-off is more important than avoiding new taxes. If not, its logic looks far less compelling. To Peterson, higher taxes and fewer benefits for the well-to-do represent the simplest common sense. But those who reject his values will resent as arrogant his assertions that "we should have been able to agree that reform must be progressive" and "we should

have been able to agree that reforming tax expenditures is a necessary part of the solution."

Undeniably, entitlement programs cost too much. Medicare's
costs have tripled since 1980; Medicaid's have quintupled. And the
future looks even grimmer. The Social Security Administration's
middle-of-the-road projections predict a 17.4-percent FICA tax by
the year 2040 and an 18.4-percent Medicare payroll tax. Since
Social Security's projections have historically underestimated the
program's actual eventual costs, it's worth dropping one's eye
down to the worst-case scenario. That scenario posits a 22.2-per-
cent FICA tax by the year 2040 and a 35.7-percent Medicare payroll tax.

As bad as those numbers are, there could be something even
worse: the wrong kind of answer to the problem of controlling
them. Kerrey, for instance, wanted to slow the increase in
Medicare spending by unilaterally reducing government payments
to doctors and hospitals. Washington has been experimenting with
this sort of medical price control since 1983, and the verdict is in:
patients get worse medicine as a result. Top-down administrative
controls do not lead health-care providers to experiment with new
types of service; health-care providers, like everyone else, only
experiment when they're under competitive pressure. In the
absence of competition, price controls tempt them into an easier
way out: water the product down. Simply deliver your captive market of optionless Medicare patients inferior medicine, in dirtier
buildings, after longer delays. It's easy, it doesn't require thinking,
and it doesn't disrupt the doctors' accustomed ways of doing business. As for the patients, where are they going to go? Canada?

Kerrey's interest in price controls underscored a harsh truth:
that the alternative to free-market entitlement reform is *not* the
unabated flow of benefits to the elderly. The real alternatives are
free-market reforms or ever-dingier and more squalid government
services. And the dinginess and squalor will be intensifying fast as
the vast baby-boom generation approaches retirement and threatens to impose nightmarish new costs on the federal Treasury.
That's why a radical Republican reform agenda is so urgently
needed now: these are the last few years in which the baby boom
generation will possess the purchasing power to make its own
retirement provisions, before its members pass sixty-five and find
themselves helplessly dependent on a deteriorating public-sector
retirement system.

The right sort of entitlement reform—the sort of reform that the Kerrey commission refused to consider—must not only liberate Washington from impossible spending commitments; it must liberate people from the Washington social-welfare system, by moving them toward individual control of their own pension and health plans. Instead of compelling hospitals to downgrade services offered to Medicare patients, Medicare could be reinvented as a system of medical savings accounts that would permit patients themselves to decide where they would economize and where they would spend. Instead of reorganizing Social Security to induce everyone to keep working to seventy, personalized tax-sheltered retirement accounts would free Americans to make their choices about when to stop working.

The details of these proposals have been floating about Washington for some time, but all of them require conservative congressmen actually to enter into the guts of America's major social welfare programs and rewrite them—a job Republicans have looked forward to with all the eagerness of a draftee getting ready to charge the barbed wire at the Somme. But the job cannot be evaded for very much longer. If one of the next three or four Congresses does not begin enacting personalized alternatives to the entitlement bureaucracies, all the Congresses after that will find themselves endlessly engaged in chop, chop, chopping the benefits paid by existing programs—or else raising payroll taxes to levels undreamt of even in Denmark or Belgium. It will be political hell: an eternity of delivering bad news to ever more insanely furious constituents. It's hard to see how the Republican congressional majority, or *any* congressional majority, can survive under those circumstances.

When the time for serious reform comes, Republicans will owe Senator Kerrey this thanks at least: he has shown them how *not* to make their case. No blue-ribbon panels, no bipartisanship. Entitlement reform is about politics, and the more ideological the politics, the better the answers it will deliver.

The "Safety Cult"

I've begun to notice something that makes me wonder whether my generation of parents isn't collectively becoming slightly insane: on my quiet residential street, the three-year-olds all wear plastic crash helmets when they ride their tricycles.

It's an amazing sight. Pedaling up and down the sidewalk, at speeds of not more than two miles per hour, little kids labor underneath protective devices that look as if they were built for cruising the highway on a Harley-Davidson.

If you combed through the annals of the insurance companies, you would find somewhere in North America an incident or possibly even two where a child tipped over his trike, landed on his head, and suffered brain damage. But it's hard to imagine that such accidents are anything remotely close to common. The parents who strap helmets onto their toddlers might reply, okay, perhaps lethal tricycle accidents do not occur very often. Why not take precautions anyway? After all, there's no such thing as being too safe.

But there *is* such a thing as being too safe. It's not just tricycle helmets. Our children are soaked with the cult of safety the way they would once have imbibed religion or patriotism. At school, teachers "street-proof" children—that is, they teach them that kidnappers and child molesters lurk in every playground. Television excites children with environmentalist fears that the air and water they breathe and drink teem with toxins, that the food they eat is saturated with deadly pesticides, and that the juice bottles they discard will soon cover the entire surface of the earth.

Their games and toys arrive with huge red warning labels on the box—that is, when they aren't prohibited outright, like the plastic walkers on wheels that toddlers love but that the safety bureaucrats have now outlawed. Elementary school children are bombarded with lectures about the perils of smoking, drugs and unsafe

141

sex; billboard ads terrify teenagers with the perils of drinking and driving. Not so long ago, the school boards drafted "peace education" curricula that described in lovingly detailed language how a nuclear explosion would cause a seven year old's skin to peel off his face.

Individually most of these campaigns are, I suppose, worthy enough. But taken together, they seem more than a little hysterical—and oppressive.

Pick up a nineteenth-century book like *Tom Sawyer,* and you can only marvel at the freedom children once had to play with penknives and pellet guns. Half a century ago, kids could buy firecrackers as freely as chewing gum. As recently as the late 1960s, responsible adults tolerated safety risks that would curl the hair of parents trained by child-care guru Penelope Leach. My family possesses a movie, filmed circa 1970, in which we kids scramble up and down a rickety metal jungle gym erected on top of uncovered paving stones. At one point, the camera stops because a child has fallen onto the stones and burst into tears; then the camera is turned back on again and the kids resume playing. It apparently occurred to nobody to move the gym.

I'll concede that some large part of the difference between Tom Sawyer's childhood, or even my own, on the one hand, and childhood today, on the other, is to the credit of the present. Adults nowadays are better informed and wiser about the risks their children run than adults used to be. But there's at least something to be said in favor of the old insouciance in the face of danger.

George Orwell observed that childhood is a time of fierce joys and fierce sorrows. Children stuff themselves with sweets at Christmas knowing perfectly well that they will be sick later because, to them, the pleasure is worth the pain.

Of course it's our job, as adults, to spoil kids' fun. Left to their own devices, they would grab carving knives and drink Javex. But it's also our job, as adults, to keep a grip on our protectiveness. Scrapes and bruises, twisted ankles, and broken legs, are the price of interesting childhoods. Parents will have more credibility when they tell their kids not to smoke if they have refrained from overexciting themselves about the perils of tricycling.

Not on My Block

During the years I lived in Toronto, I took my daughter to nursery school by subway. Perhaps that does not sound so very remarkable, but to a former New Yorker such as myself, remarkable is the only word for it. Nobody who could help it would take a child onto the New York subway, with its deranged beggars, drying pools of urine, and advertisements urging teenagers to use condoms.

But while Toronto still remains "Toronto the Good" below ground, things are quite different above. When we emerge from the train at the corner on which her school is located, we walk out directly underneath a three-story-high poster of a nearly naked young man in a very visible state of semi-excitement inside his Calvin Klein briefs. The picture is the latest installment of one of the most successful advertising campaigns in history. It is also a direct attack on the wholesomeness of my child's environment.

What makes the poster all the more amazing is that the rules, regulations, and informal codes that govern advertising in Toronto and elsewhere in Canada are normally so strict. It would, for example, be very, very illegal to put up a billboard reading: "People have been enjoying wine in moderation for centuries. Have a glass with dinner," because advertising may not promote drinking in preference to nondrinking. It violates the law to put up a photograph of the Marlboro Man—even if fully clothed. To stay on the careful side of the regulation forbidding them to appeal to young people, beer makers refrain from using actors under the age of twenty-five in their commercials.

Finally, and although it entirely lacks the legal authority to do so, the Ontario government since 1990 has made it clear to all liquor advertisers that if they want to avoid trouble, they'll purge their print and broadcast commercials of anything that the government in its super-sensitivity deems "sexist." No Swedish bikini teams for Canadian beer drinkers.

The rules for advertising products other than alcohol and tobacco are laxer. But they are not all that lax. You need a permit to put up a billboard, and the planning authorities possess wide discretion over whether to grant or refuse the permit. And even once a permit has been granted, the advertiser remains subject to the ordinary law of the province: which means, among other things, that he must obey the Ontario Human Rights Code. As that code is now interpreted, it's doubtful whether the Klein company would win a human rights challenge if it had displayed an equivalently explicit ad featuring a woman.

It should seem odd to everyone that we have to rely on human rights codes to keep sexual images off our billboards. We use bylaws, not human rights codes, to stop sound trucks from driving through residential neighborhoods blaring, "Buy Calvin Klein underwear!" We use bylaws to forbid smoking in places where the smell of cigarettes might annoy nonsmokers. We use bylaws to prevent city residents from keeping smelly animals in their backyards. Why can't we use bylaws to suppress the nuisance of lurid billboards? Canadian law recognizes only the most minimal free speech rights even for decent advertisements—why then should we be bashful about controlling advertising when it is indecent?

When the U.S. Supreme Court began to liberalize American obscenity law in the late 1950s and early 1960s, it made a point of drawing distinctions between different types of media. What was protected by the First Amendment's guarantee of free speech when enclosed within the cloth covers of a book was not necessarily protected when emblazoned on a movie marquee. Some forms of expression can be escaped; others—billboards, sound trucks, posters—cannot. The second group can therefore reasonably be more strictly regulated.

Later, more liberal, courts rejected this line of argument, but it still makes sense: nobody ever has to read any particular book, but the users of a street corner are willy-nilly subjected to messages slapped up there. It seems an appropriate function of municipal government to use its police powers to keep those messages clean—at least as appropriate a function as waging endless war against the largely mythical dangers of secondhand smoke.

Not This Quagmire

Liberia, Somalia, Bosnia, Haiti, Rwanda. Since the end of the Cold War, the Western world has been confronted with a series of human disasters that seem to demand our help. And yet, when we do help—as we did in Somalia—the results disappoint everyone. What ought people of conscience to think?

Our moral duty is clear: we must do what we can. If it is in our power to deliver food and water to people who would otherwise suffer and die, we must. But another thing is clear too: our duty to help is limited.

The hundreds of thousands (the newspapers say millions, but be cautious: nobody is counting, and the aid workers who are the source for such numbers are naturally tempted to choose the biggest imaginable figure) of Rwandans who fled their country didn't want our water, powdered milk and surplus sorghum—or they didn't want it for very long, anyway. They wanted to go home. Very reasonably, they will not go home until they feel confident their home is safe. In this case, the refugees—most of whom are Hutu—will wait until they know that the new Tutsi-controlled government of Rwanda will not seek revenge for the massacres of Tutsi tribespeople by the army of the previous Hutu-controlled government.

It would theoretically be possible, of course, for the Western world—meaning, principally, the United States—to create such confidence. The U.S. and its allies could take control of the country and enforce peace. Then they could appoint a new government made up of the least-bloodthirsty people in the country, recruit, arm, and train a new army for the new government, and leave Western troops there for whatever length of time it took the new authorities to consolidate their rule. At the time of the Somali adventure, many intelligent commentators argued that this sort of

145

neo-colonial protectorship was exactly what Africa needed. The British historian Paul Johnson then wrote, "[The belief that] all peoples are ready for independence . . . has been proved illusory, at incalculable cost in human misery."

And perhaps Johnson is right. But does the fact that Africa needs neo-colonialism mean that the West must provide it? Does our duty to relieve misery extend this far?

A lot of people in comfortable Western countries are tempted to say "yes." I wonder whether we will feel the same way when Western troops occupy half a dozen countries south of the Sahara, propping up their regimes, drilling their armies, policing their countrysides.

When Europeans divided up the African continent in the late nineteenth century, the place had achieved a level of political development roughly equivalent to late medieval Europe. There were a few powerful kingdoms in the north and west; elsewhere, the largest unit of government was an agglomeration of villages. The Europeans left only seventy-five years later, but they bequeathed Africa all the apparatus of the modern state—bureaucracies, professional armies, mechanisms of economic control. They drew lines on the map, called the areas inside the lines "Rwanda" or "Zambia," and expected "Rwanda" and "Zambia" to function more or less the way Britain and France did. Unsurprisingly, the experiment quickly failed.

Now Africa is in the process of rejecting colonialism's last artificial grafts. It is moving back in time, to its own past, to local authority, and unceasing war. Unfortunately, two other European introductions—modern weapons and nationalist ideology—guarantee that Africa's post-colonial conflicts will be waged with far greater ruthlessness and exponentially greater suffering than in pre-colonial days. Relieving the worst of that suffering is the duty of foreign onlookers.

To stop that suffering from recurring, however, will require the imposition of a new system of authority on the continent. Better to wait the decades it may take for the Africans to impose it upon themselves than for us to do it for them.

Even Canada Needs the Bomb

Whenever a world crisis erupts, it's easy to spot the Canadian foreign minister: he's the man demanding a special session of the United Nations. In matters great and small, from the invasion of Afghanistan to the death threat against Salman Rushdie, Canada seems always to take the prissiest line in the Western world. This doesn't do the Western world much harm—who listens?—but it's not very gratifying to national pride.

But then, national pride never seems to have much influenced Canadian foreign and defense policy. Throughout their country's history, Canadians have relied on others to take care of them: first the British, then the Americans. In renouncing the obligation of self-defense, Canada has refused to discharge for itself the one responsibility that no state can ever fully entrust to another. This must once have seemed like a clever money-saving idea, but over the years the seeping psychic costs of taking shelter behind the warships, troops, and missiles of someone else have gnawed at the country's always fragile self-esteem.

Canada has tried to compensate for this military dependency by erecting cultural and economic barriers to foreign influence. It hasn't worked. The trouble with Canada is not that it doesn't produce its own television shows, but that it doesn't defend its own borders. This is what has made Canada's forty-five-year-old decision to deny itself nuclear weapons so consequential. The bomb is the decisive weapon of our epoch. Without it, Canada must forever hide behind the strength of others. That hurts. And asserting national sovereignty in oil-drilling and publishing and all the areas where it does not belong cannot begin to remedy the failure to assert sovereignty in the one area where it does.

Canada is no nuclear virgin. Canada's contributions to the invention of the atomic bomb are largely forgotten now, but they did not go unnoticed at the time. President Truman, not a man for empty compliments, described Canada and Great Britain as "our associates in this discovery" in his first formal message to Congress on the atomic bomb, on October 3, 1945. Canadian scientists at Chalk River in Quebec manufactured the heavy water for the atomic bombs dropped on Hiroshima and Nagasaki. The uranium that formed their explosive cores was mined in Canada. Prime Minister Mackenzie King had been briefed on the Manhattan project on July 15, 1942—the first world leader after Churchill to get the news. While Canada did not know all the secrets of the atomic bomb at the end of the war, it knew almost as much as Great Britain, and more than the Soviet Union. The mission of the Soviet spy ring exposed by defector Igor Gouzenko was the infiltration of Chalk River.

Not only did Canada assist in the development of the American bomb, and supply many of its raw materials, but Canadian troops used to be equipped with nuclear weapons. Until 1972, the Canadian forces in Europe deployed battlefield nuclear artillery, and nuclear-tipped Bomarc missiles guarded Montreal and Toronto against Soviet bombers from 1963 until 1972. American nuclear delivery systems, like the cruise missile, have been tested here, and nuclear-armed American ships and aircraft dock in our ports and land at our airbases.

Still, this history of involvement with nuclear weapons does not really call into question Canada's status as a non-nuclear power. Canada never fielded an *independent* nuclear deterrent. The warheads Canada deployed were made in the United States and were always subject to American control. In peacetime they were kept under American lock and key; in war, the order to fire them would have had to come from an American officer.

After the war, the nuclear technology that Canada had helped invent was rapidly diffused. The Soviet Union tested an atomic bomb of its own in 1949. Britain followed in 1952. Later in 1952, the Americans upped the ante by detonating a thermonuclear "hydrogen" bomb with many times the destructive power of those used on Hiroshima and Nagasaki. The Soviets caught up in 1953; Great Britain in 1957. China exploded a thermonuclear device in 1965, France in 1968, and India in 1974. Israel seems to have acquired the bomb in the early 1970s. Twenty-five years after the end of the Second World War, every one of the world's top economic powers that had not been on the losing side of the war possessed the bomb—except for Canada.

This is strange behavior. Why *wouldn't* a state acquire the most powerful weapons it could afford? Especially a state that is not quite a major power? The bomb is, after all, a great equalizer. In 1939, a middle power like Czechoslovakia or Poland could hope to stand up to a great power like Germany or the Soviet Union for a few weeks at best. Now, a nuclear-armed middle power like France can convincingly threaten to inflict terrible devastation on a superpower—not comparable, certainly, to what the superpower could do to France, but ghastly enough to cause the superpower to hesitate before an act of aggression. Nuclear nations, even quite small ones like Israel, can act with a self-assurance unimaginable to the most powerful of non-nuclear states—Japan, for example, or West Germany. Canada's behavior is stranger still, because it has not only deprived itself of nuclear arms, but of conventional strength as well. The 2.1 percent of the gross domestic product Canada spends on the military has bought a navy of twenty three warships, an ill-equipped army, and a tiny, overextended air force.

As with many of the more embarrassing incidents in Canada's diplomatic history, the explanation lies in the peculiarities of the External Affairs mandarins who devised Canada's role in the postwar world. These men have dazzled two generations of high school textbook writers with their adept imitations of English manners, costume, and accent; their subtle manoeuvrings at the United Nations; their artful softening of NATO communiqués; their self-congratulatory idealism; their intricate memoranda on the opportunities for honest-brokerage; and their lingering presence in the background while houseboys served cocktails at surreptitious meetings of American and Chinese diplomats. But despite their innumerable learned degrees, these men—the "smooth Canadians who haunt the corridors of Washington with their confidential ineffective briefs," as historian James Eayrs called them—never quite figured out how the game was played.

Their master, Mackenzie King, piously reproved conservatives in his diary because "they do not rely on international friendships. They rely only on force and power. Force and power bring force and power to oppose them." And so his underlings believed. The celebrated mandarins of External Affairs never relied on force and power. To the suppressed amusement of the Americans and Europeans, Canada insisted on inserting a section on cultural and social affairs in the NATO treaty, lest the Russians get the idea that the new alliance intended to rely on force and power. Norman Robertson, then Canada's top foreign policy official, urged the Americans to share the bomb with the Soviets to enhance peace and international understanding. At the Truman-Attlee-King summit of 1945, future prime minister Lester Pearson piped up that "we could prevent global catastrophe only by global agreement of an unprecedented character." As far as the written record shows, in all their thousands of hours of anxious meditation about the bomb, it never occurred to any of these highly sophisticated men that Canada might want one for itself. Did they perhaps speculate that Canada's position in the world might be secured by the cleverness of its diplomats and the benevolence of its intentions? Did they fear the bomb so much that they felt safer with it in anybody's hands but their own? Did they feel so little pride in Canada's war effort that they did not feel they were entitled to a permanent place of honour in the post-war world? Or were they so confident of the gratitude of the greater powers for Dieppe and the Battle of the Atlantic that they thought no further effort necessary to preserve their place?

In any case, the possibility of acquiring nuclear weapons was so alien to them that Canada can hardly be said to have ever made a positive decision *not* to build a bomb. In all the memoirs of the period, the only reference I can find to any consideration of the possibility is an aside in George Ignatieff's *The Making of a Peacemonger:* before the Quebec Conference of 1943, Mackenzie King "had already decided that Canada was only interested in atomic energy for peaceful purposes." King's diaries (as edited by Jack Pickersgill) never discuss this momentous subject. Canada accepted a position in the third tier of nations, below the superpowers and the nuclear middle powers, without question or demur.

Why? When Charles de Gaulle assumed the presidency of France in 1959, it was a poorer and less technologically advanced country than Canada. But de Gaulle insisted on strict equality with the superpowers, and his utterly unrealistic determination that France be treated as a nation of the first rank propelled her from the third into the second. Ever since, France has been strikingly immune to the periodic outbursts of anxiety common in the rest of Europe. In the Great Nuclear Fear of 1982, France was the only country in the West not afflicted by a mass unilateral disarmament movement: not just because the French instinctively know that *any-*

thing that gets a million Germans marching in the streets is a bad idea, but also because in France, as nowhere else in Europe, the bomb is a symbol of national independence, not of subordination to the United States.

The Americans have always objected to the acquisition of nuclear weapons by their allies, in part to preserve their own hegemony, in part because they believe that allies who have defense money to spend should spend them on tanks and aircraft. Although the British had helped immeasurably in the creation of the American bomb, and although Roosevelt had promised Churchill at Quebec that the United States would consult Great Britain before using the bomb, the U.S. Congress cut off atomic cooperation as soon as the war ended. The British built their first bombs on their own; they got American help for their maintenance of a thermonuclear arsenal only because the supple Harold Macmillan massaged the credulity and anglophilia of Jack Kennedy. The French and Israeli bombs were built in the teeth of unrelenting American hostility. The haughty de Gaulle fearlessly stood up to the Americans; and the Israelis, surrounded by mortal enemies, are not disposed to listen to anybody. But Canada—well, Canada anticipated the American reaction.

It would have been especially difficult for Canada to withstand American pressures (had an atomic project ever begun) because it would not have been easy to articulate a strategic doctrine for a Canadian nuclear force. The nuclear arsenal of the United States does a more than adequate job of deterring Soviet attacks on North America, so what precisely would a Canadian bomb do that an American bomb does not already do better and more cheaply? And the answer, of course, is nothing. The strategic ramifications of a Canadian deterrent would be identical to those of an American deterrent, with a single difference: the ultimate means of Canada's national defence would rest in Canadian hands.

Canada has never clearly thought through how much independence in its foreign policy it can reasonably maintain. The Atlanticist school of thought, which was almost universal in Canada until the Vietnam War, and which has continued to predominate, holds the country's freedom to be quite limited. As a small nation beside a hugely powerful one, Canada had better not cross the United States on anything it really cares about. This way of thinking induced Liberal party leader Lester Pearson to flip-flop in 1963, when he suddenly changed his mind about putting American-controlled nuclear warheads atop the Bomarc missiles the Conservative Diefenbaker government had purchased. The opposing, nationalist point of view that has spread since the middle sixties, insists that Canada could safely dissent from the Americans on issues relating to the Soviet Union and the Third World.

Weirdly, the apparently more pro-American school, the Atlanticist one, is more afraid of the United States than the anti-American one. The opinion of the nationalists was articulated in their seminal collection of essays, *An Independent Foreign Policy for Canada?:* "The danger of anything deserving the name retaliation is minimal. 'Pressure,' yes; 'retaliation,' no." Like true children of the sixties, the nationalists knew that the authorities they were defying would not smack them. The older generation wasn't so sure.

Yet there was always something unreal about the debate between the Atlanticists and the nationalists. The proposals for an independent foreign policy floated by the nationalists never dwelt very long on Canada's particular needs and circumstances. In fact, they bore a curious resemblance to the previous week's editorial in *The Nation.* If the ideas of the Atlanticists were neo-colonial borrowings from Dean Acheson and Dean Rusk, the ideas of the nationalists were neo-colonial borrowings from Henry Wallace and Gabriel Kolko. Assessing Canada's interests in the world, and then creating the necessary means for securing them, would have entailed, at the very least, an effective intelligence service and military sufficiency. This never captured the nationalists' imagination. They believed independence to be a matter of making speeches, taking tea with African guerilla leaders, and voting at the U.N. They worried as little about laying the material basis for exploring the limits of our independence as the Atlanticists. Intellectually, they mimicked the American left even more slavishly than the Atlanticists followed the American Center. Neither faction troubled to peer out from under the American nuclear umbrella at a stormy world beyond.

Canada has developed a number of attractive but implausible justifications for not having nuclear weapons. The one most often heard in official circles is that Canada is setting a good example for the principle of non-proliferation. Admirable, perhaps, but the world is not inclined to follow Canada's lead. When Mackenzie King vetoed a Canadian bomb, there were only two atomic powers on the horizon, the United States and Great Britain. Today there are at least fifteen nuclear or near-nuclear states. Countries acquire or refrain from acquiring weapons out of consideration of their interests, not because they are inspired by superior moral example: states, as de Gaulle observed, are rather inhuman monsters. Anyway, Canada's contribution to nuclear non-proliferation is a touch more—shall we say ambiguous—than official self-congratulators will admit. Canada supplied India with the raw materials and technology to make its bomb, although India had not signed the non-proliferation treaty (and still hasn't). When Israel, in the only successful enforcement of the principle of non-proliferation, bombed the Iraqi nuclear reactor at Osirak, Canada voted with a majority of the United Nations to condemn her.

Related to this justification is another, more popular thirty years ago than now. Peace-loving Canada, it was said—most fervently by Prime Minister Diefenbaker's external affairs minister, the gooey Howard Green—was in a unique position to win the respect and admiration of the newly decolonized nations of Africa and Asia. At the time, this was widely considered to be something worth having. But even if it were, it's hard to win the respect of others by failing to do what they themselves would wish to do. Virtually every Third World country with the money and know-how—Brazil, Pakistan, Argentina, Iraq, Egypt, Taiwan, and South Korea, to cite the most prominent—has tried, or is trying now, to build itself a bomb. India and China have succeeded. And yet all of these states have had the benefit of innumerable improving lectures from idealistic Canadians. Psychology, not politics, explains why the people who run Canada are so peculiarly prone to attributing supreme moral virtue to the despots and dictators of backward countries.

Popular opinion has had a more basic reason for opposing a Canadian bomb: the conviction, or hope, that the Russians will be less likely to bomb Canada if Canada cannot bomb them. It is true that nothing on Canadian soil is so urgent a Soviet target as the missile fields of North Dakota, or the submarine pens of Norfolk, Virginia, and Puget Sound, Washington. But what little we know of Soviet nuclear strategy suggests that if North Dakota gets hit first, Canadian targets get hit two minutes later. Once they make the awful decision to use nuclear weapons, they will not intend to restrict their attack to the enemy's warheads; they will mean to devastate his total warmaking power. Few places contribute more to NATO's warmaking power than the industrial complex that stretches around the western edge of Lake Ontario from Oshawa, Ontario, to

Rochester, New York.. The Russians will not be inclined to spare the northern two-thirds of the complex because it happens to fly a red and white flag instead of a red, white, and blue one.

As the postwar order slowly dissolves, the time for a reconsideration of Canada's defense posture approaches. Soviet leader Mikhail Gorbachev seems to be trying to do two things: to ease the imperial burdens upon the Soviet Union and to remove some of the ideology from its struggle with the United States. If he succeeds, human beings will not be suddenly cured of aggression. Nor will Canada's location under the missile paths of the two greatest world powers change. If anything, the dissolution of the big ideological blocs could make the world a more unpleasant place. When democracy confronted totalitarianism across the Elbe, Canada could feel no choice but to enlist as a junior partner in the democratic alliance. In a five-cornered tussle between Western Europe, America, China, Japan, and Russia, it's every state for itself. A world in which nations jockey free-lance for position, in which many Third World states—Brazil, for example, or India—combine modern weapons systems with hot-blooded national ambitions, is not necessarily going to be safer, or kinder, than the world of the Cold War.

At the moment, Canada will not correct Mackenzie King's mistake. So long as the basic arrangements of the postwar order linger, Canada will retain the place it chose in 1945. But when that order vanishes, what should Canada do?

The defense strategy of the Mulroney government, which directs Canada's expenditures away from its land forces to the navy, is fine, as far as it goes. The Europeans hardly need Canada to supply their infantry for them. And the emphasis on submarines is right too: if the surface warship isn't quite obsolete yet, it will be by the end of the century.

But none of this amounts to an independent military capacity. Independence requires the power, on one's own, to hurt an aggressor. Until Canada acquires its own nuclear deterrent, it will be a ward of its allies.

A Trident submarine, which is the most survivable nuclear launch pad, can carry up to a hundred and twenty small but very accurate nuclear warheads. A Canadian government that took its rhetoric of independence seriously might look into buying three or four: enough to frighten off any international bully without asking for help. In the coming season of détente, it may be possible to buy them secondhand.

PART III

Books and Thinkers

Living Without the
Many Pages of My Life

At the beginning of 1994, my family and I returned to Toronto for two years after more than five years in New York. The move has been even more turbulent than moves usually are, and for some three months most of our possessions were locked up in a storage depot, waiting for their new home. For me, the worst of it was living without my books.

It's an odd thing that living without one's old books should be so troubling. The vast majority of the books on my shelves go far longer than three months without being touched. They were bought and read two or three or ten years ago: why should a three-month separation from them now cause me any distress?

And yet it is distressing. I had had ten different addresses since graduation from college, and I was about to move into my eleventh. Until very recently, I never owned much in the way of furniture. The only constant things in all these different apartments and houses were the fifty or so crates of books I carted from one place to another. Because I file my books the same way—alphabetically by author's name, a system enforced with near-neurotic rigidity—they always stare out at me in the same order, making every new home instantly familiar.

By very rough estimate, my books together weigh about three thousand pounds. When you haul a ton and a half of books every year or every other year, you do find yourself wondering why anyone bothers to own books at all. How many books bear reading more than once? When finished, why not just give or throw them away?

I can't claim to have formulated a completely satisfactory answer. One justification is that a personal library makes it easy to lay hands on information when you need it. Did John A. Macdonald die in 1891 or 1892? How does the last line in "Ode to a Nightingale" go? It's convenient not to have to toss on a coat and trudge to the public library every time you cannot remember something.

Not, however, convenient enough to justify the enormous trouble caused by keeping up a library of one's own. The real answer, I'm afraid, lies a little deeper in the oddities of the psyche. Many—actually, to be truthful, probably the majority—of the formative experiences of my life were books rather than actions. I keep my books for the same reason that an athlete keeps his old football or a woman her engagement ring: they are the physical record of a crucial event. I still own the battered paperback edition of *The Scarlet Pimpernel* I read and re-read as a boy on the Greyhound bus from my parents' house in Toronto to my grandparents' in Niagara Falls. When my eye falls on it, I can once again smell diesel, and see in my mind the face of my late grandfather waiting at the station as the bus pulled in. And I wonder: how much of the conservatism of my adult politics can be traced to the hatred of the French Revolution that wafted through the pages of Baroness Orczy's swashbuckling romance?

My books represent my aspirations as well as my past. Interspersed among the geniuses—among the Shakespeares, Prousts, and Gibbons—are the books that contain the lesser achievements that lie within the reach of more ordinary talents. When I glance at them, I see the work that other writers have been able to do when they exerted themselves. And I am forced to ask myself, am I trying as hard as I can? Am I doing my best to live up to the standards of the writers I admire?

When one walks into the room of someone who owns a lot of books, it's an irresistible temptation to sidle up to the shelves, and evaluate what is there. In some ways, this is a rude habit: certainly I feel nosy when I do it, just as I feel self-conscious whenever anyone looks over my shelves—so much so, in fact, that I try to put my books in the bedroom, the halls, anywhere except the living room.

Still, when someone has furnished his room with the same objects with which he has furnished his mind, it's almost impossible not to look. Show me your books, and I will know who you are. And if I have so laboriously transported my books from Toronto to Boston to New York, back to Toronto, and then on again, perhaps the real truth is that I do it to remind myself of who I am.

The Legacy of
Russell Kirk

Russell Kirk, who died this spring at his home in Mecosta, Michigan, at the age of seventy-five, has left behind an intellectual and literary achievement as huge as it is difficult to categorize. He was not exactly a political theorist, nor really a philosopher, certainly not a historian; and yet his work speaks profound truths about politics, philosophy, and history. An ardent enemy of Communism, he was barely more enthusiastic about the commercial civilization of America. An unrelenting critic of "King Numbers," he championed a Goldwaterite conservatism that owed far more to the populism of Jefferson, Jackson, and Tom Paine than to the prescriptive politics of Edmund Burke and John Adams. A scourge of ideology and abstraction in politics, he determinedly refused to pay any attention to the circumstances and context in which the thinkers he studied had lived. He loved old cathedral towns and country fields, ancient mansions and Gothic universities; he hated cars, television, and shopping malls. For all his patriotism, one has to wonder how comfortable he ever really felt in late-twentieth-century America. "Against the lust for change," Kirk wrote of his admired John Randolph, "[he] had fought with all his talents. And though he lost, he fell with a brilliancy that was almost consolation for disaster." Of course, it wasn't just Randolph he had in mind.

Russell Kirk came of one of the many small-town families hit hard by the Depression. His great-grandfather had founded the little town of Mecosta, and his mother's father had owned a bank, but Kirk attended Michigan State on a scholarship and worked at Ford's Rouge River plant after completing his M.A. at Duke in 1941. Kirk was then drafted and stationed in Utah; according to

George Nash, author of *The Conservative Intellectual Tradition in America Since 1945*, Kirk cast his first presidential ballot for Norman Thomas in 1944, to reward the veteran socialist for his steadfast opposition to the Second World War. Released from the army, Kirk resumed his studies and began to publish. In 1951 came *John Randolph of Roanoke*, an enlargement of his M.A. thesis, and in 1953, *The Conservative Mind*. The fame that second book won Kirk enabled him to return to Mecosta and settle in his family's house.

A charming 1992 essay by Edwin Feulner, president of the Heritage Foundation, quotes Kirk's description of the place: "over everything brooded an air of faded splendours, vanished lands, and baffled expectations." The house soon sheltered armies of young conservative scholars, and other, more miscellaneous, guests: "unwed mothers, half-reformed burglars, . . . Vietnamese . . . families, waves of Ethiopians, Poles fled from martial law, freedom-seeking Croats, students disgusted with their colleges, and a diversity of waifs and strays from Progress." (The sarcastic upper-case "P" on "Progress" is a characteristic Kirkean flourish.)

From Mecosta, for four decades, Kirk fired his observations upon the world: two more major scholarly works, *Eliot and His Age* and *The Roots of American Order*, books, essays, ghost stories, lectures, columns for magazines and newspapers. From Mecosta too he cast a sharp and often disapproving eye upon the conservative movement that had sprung up in the years since the publication of *The Conservative Mind*. He disliked libertarians, and apologists for big business, and neoconservatives. He did not mind making enemies: he separated himself from his old friends at *National Review* after 1980, and in a 1988 critique of neoconservatism he let loose the startling observation that "not seldom has it seemed as if some eminent Neoconservatives"—that capital letter again!—"mistook Tel Aviv for the capital of the United States." By the end of his life, he had circled back to his Taftite origins, and joined the opposition to the war in the Persian Gulf.

Kirk's voice echoed less powerfully in those later years than in the 1950s and 1960s. In part, of course, he was the victim of his own success: with conservatives in a position to exercise national political power after 1978, a political thinker who declined to preoccupy himself with the details of public policy—which he left to the "enlightened expediency" of statesmen—inevitably lost audiences to technical experts. Clad in out-of-fashion vested suits, immersed in his old books, smoking (as Feulner says) "dark, thick Burmese cigars that looked and tasted like torpedoes," he looked oddly out of place among the sleek Republicans of Reagan-era Washington.

And these stylistic oddities hinted at an even bigger and deeper gulf between Kirk and his Reaganite audience. From the beginning, Kirk had denied key tenets of the American faith. He had openly defended class hierarchies; he doubted the value of technological progress; and, while disliking the growth of the central government, he cared very little for the danger to prosperity and economic growth posed by bigger government. In fact, Kirk regarded "growth," in most cases, as a misnomer for "decay."

> During the late 'fifties and the early 'sixties, I watched in Long Island the devastation of what had been a charming countryside, as dismaying as what was being done to our cities. To make room for a spreading population was necessary: but to do it hideously and stupidly was not ineluctable. Much of the mischief was accomplished by the highways of Robert Moses, generally supposed to be one of the abler of American planners. Speed was everything, speed by automobile from Manhattan to Montauk.

Many thinkers have damned suburbia, but Kirk uniquely dared to reveal the anti-egalitarian implications of the aesthetic critique of American life. "This is my case: there ought to be inequality of condition in the world. For without inequality, there is no class; without class, no manners and no beauty; and then a people sink into public and private ugliness." Ugliness was for him no light accusation. "With Santayana," he said, "I believe that beauty is the index to civilization." By this index, contemporary America scored low. We now live, he bitterly complained in *The Conservative Mind*, in "a world smudged by industrialism, standardized by the masses, consolidated by government."

Nor was Kirk bashful about itemizing the differences between his conservatism and the enthusiastic Jacksonianism found on the right wing of the contemporary Republican Party. He openly disdained populism, denouncing "those who, in the belief that there exists a malign 'elite' cry, with Carl Sandburg, 'The people, yes!'" As for the Reagan-era project of identifying conservatism's cause as the defense of "democratic capitalism," an optimistic philosophy that commingled high-tech prosperity and ever-widening popular sovereignty . . . well, here's what Kirk had to say about that:

Previously, even in America, the structure of society had consisted of a hierarchy of personal and local allegiances—man to master, apprentice to preceptor, householder to parish or town, constituent to representative, son to father, communicant to church. . . . This network of personal relationships and local decencies was brushed aside by steam, coal, the spinning jenny, the cotton gin, speedy transportation, and the other items in that catalogue of progress which school children memorize. The Industrial Revolution . . . turned the world inside out. Personal loyalties gave way to financial relationships. . . . Industrialism was a harder knock to conservatism than the books of the French equalitarians. . . .

That the sudden triumph of democracy should coincide with the rise of industrialism was in part the product of intertwined causes; but, however inescapable, it was a conjunction generally catastrophic. Jeffersonian democracy, designed for a simple agrarian people, was thrust upon an acquisitive, impatient, and often urbanized mass of men.

Instead, Kirk throughout his life insisted upon the six "canons" of conservative thought he first identified in *The Conservative Mind:*

1. Belief that a divine intent rules society as well as conscience. . . .
2. Affection for the proliferating variety and mystery of traditional life. . . .
3. Conviction that civilized society requires orders and classes. . . .
4. Persuasion that property and freedom are inseparably connected. . . .
5. Faith in prescription. . . . Tradition and sound prejudice provide checks upon man's anarchic impulse. . . .
6. Recognition that change and reform are not identical, and that innovation is a devouring conflagration more often than it is a torch of progress. . . .

Kirk expressed his major ideas in highly general terms, and so it is hard to know exactly what these six canons imply, especially the final two. When pressed for specifics, Kirk's political advice tended to take the form of negative injunctions.

Conservative people in politics need to steer clear of the Scylla of abstraction and the Charybdis of opportunism. So it is that folk of conservative inclination ought to decline the embraces of such categories of American political zealots or charlatans as I list below:

Those who demand that the National Parks be sold to private developers. Those who declare that "the test of the market" is the whole of political economy and of morals. Those who fancy that foreign policy can be conducted with religious zeal on a basis of absolute rights and absolute wrongs. . . .

Etcetera. Even Kirk's journalism bears only indirectly on the controversies of his day.

Then again, uncertainty about the implications of his ideas in practice may not matter very much: for Kirk was, at bottom, much more concerned with morals and education than with politics as politics is usually understood. He reserved his energies for other themes, themes sometimes absurdly small, but at other times profound and urgent, as in his remarkable essay "The Rarity of the God-Fearing Man."

"We have to begin," Kirk describes himself telling a group of clergymen, "with the dogma that the fear of God is the beginning of wisdom." "Oh no," they replied, "not the *fear* of God. You mean the *love* of God, don't you?"

Looking upon their mild and diffident faces, I wondered how much trust I might put in such love as they knew. Their meekness was not that of Moses. Meek before Jehovah, Moses had no fear of Pharaoh; but these doctors of the schools, much at ease in Zion, were timid in the presence of a traffic policeman. Although convinced that God is too indulgent to punish much of anything, they were given to trembling before Caesar. . . . Gauleiters and commissars? Why, their fellowship and charity was not proof against a dean or a divisional head. . . .

Every age portrays God in the image of its poetry and its politics. In one century, God is an absolute monarch, exacting his due; in another century, still an absolute sovereign, but a benevolent despot; again, perhaps a grand gentleman among aristocrats; at a different time, a democratic president, with an eye to the ballot box. It has been said that to many of our generation, God is a Republican and works in a bank; but this image is giving way, I think, to God as Chum—at worst, God as a playground supervisor. . . .

In a Michigan college town stands an immense quasi-Gothic church building, and the sign upon the porch informs the world that this is "The People's Church, Nondenominational and Non-sectarian." Sometimes, passing by, a friend of mine murmurs, "The People's Church—formerly God's" . . . From the People's Church, the fear of God, with its allied wisdom, has been swept away. So have I.

Kirk's literary productivity commands awe. He took particular pride in his ghost stories: his spare curriculum vitae modestly omits mention of nearly all his innumerable awards and honorary degrees, except for three that especially pleased him—one of them being the Ann Radcliffe Award of the Count Dracula Society. ("A child's fearful joy in stories of goblins, witches, and ghosts is a natural yearning after the challenge of the dreadful: raw head and bloody bones, in one form or another, the imagination demands.") In all the millions of words he set in print, however, he never amended or retracted any of the thoughts and formulations of the masterpiece he published at age thirty-two, *The Conservative Mind*.

"Professor J. W. Williams kindly read the manuscript of this book; and in his library at the Roundel, looking upon the wreck of St. Andrews cathedral, we talked of the inundation which only here and there has spared an island of humane learning like St. Andrews town." Those words, the opening sentence of the acknowledgments to *The Conservative Mind*, and the first of Russell Kirk's that most of his readers will encounter, demonstrate what a fine literary artist he could be. You might close the book right there, and Kirk would already have stabbed you with a pang of loss and regret. An old cliché has it that a great actor can wring tears our of audience by reading a laundry list. Kirk could summon up nostalgia with a list of place-names. "These chapters have been written in a variety of places: in a but-and-ben snuggled under the cliffs of Eigg; in one of the ancient towers of Kellie Castle, looking out to the Forth; in my great-grandfather's house in the stump-country of Michigan; among the bogs of Sligo in the west of Ireland; upon the steps of Ara Coeli, in Rome; at Balcarres House, where what Burke calls 'the unbought grace of life' still abides."

Kirk was writing in the aftermath of the forty most catastrophic years in the history of Western civilization, and at the beginning of another forty of the most tense and terrifying. It must have seemed to him that everything he treasured had either been pulverized by

war or would soon be bulldozed by one form of
another. He strained all his powers to summon up a vi
Anglo-American past that would stir the imagination, and
to preserve as much of the vanished aristocratic age he love
possibly could. In form, *The Conservative Mind* appears to be
lectual history. Each of its chapters closely studies the writing of a
conservative thinker or group of thinkers: Edmund Burke; John
Adams, Alexander Hamilton, and Fisher Ames; Walter Scott and
Samuel Taylor Coleridge; Benjamin Disraeli and Cardinal New-
man; Irving Babbitt and George Santayana; and many others. In
fact, history is the one thing *The Conservative Mind* is not. Kirk
repeatedly declares his lack of interest in the tangle of facts and
events from which his subjects' ideas emerged. He takes his ideas
as he finds them, the way an anthropologist might examine an arti-
fact, or a New Critic, a poem. Was John C. Calhoun's dramatic
midlife switch from nationalism to sectionalism motivated by his
commitment to slavery? Kirk does not inquire.

> The whole grim slavery-problem, to which no satisfactory answer
> was possible, warped and discolored the American political mind,
> on either side of the debate, for the earlier two-thirds of the nine-
> teenth century. So far as it is possible, we shall try to keep clear
> here of that partisan controversy over slavery and to penetrate,
> instead, beneath the froth of abolitionist harangues and Southern
> fire-caring to those conservative ideas which Randolph and Cal-
> houn enunciated.

Are we really to take Benjamin Disraeli's flights of political fancy
seriously as expressing a distinctive Tory philosophy? It doesn't
matter whether we do.

> In truth, Disraeli's positive legislation sometimes was inconsistent
> with his theory, and in any case inferior to it. His really important
> achievement, as a political leader, was implanting in the public
> imagination an ideal of Toryism which has been immeasurably
> valuable in keeping Britain faithful to her constitutional and spiri-
> tual traditions.

No, *The Conservative Mind* isn't history; it is a work of literature
meant to achieve political ends.

This isn't to deny that Kirk could produce acute analysis of
earlier times when it suited his purposes. Kirk's erasure of Alexan-

der Hamilton—the hero of an earlier generation of conservative Republicans—from the conservative canon shows his historical intelligence at its best.

> It hardly seems to have occurred to Hamilton's mind that a con-solidated nation might also be a levelling and innovating nation, though he had the example of Jacobin France right before him; and he does not appear to have reflected on the possibility that force in government may be applied to other purposes than the maintenance of a conservative order.... All his revolutionary ardour notwithstanding, Hamilton loved English society as an English colonial adores it. His vision of the coming America was of another, stronger, richer, eighteenth-century England. . . .
>
> [T]hat industrialization of America which Hamilton success-fully promoted was burdened with consequences the haughty and forceful new aristocrat did not perceive. Commerce and manu-factures, he believed, would produce a body of wealthy men whose interests would coincide with those of the national com-monwealth. Probably he conceived of these pillars of society as being very like great English merchants—purchasing country estates, forming presently a stable class possessed of leisure, tal-ent, and means, providing moral and political and intellectual leadership for the nation. The actual American businessman, gen-erally speaking, has turned out to be a different sort of person: it is difficult to reproduce social classes from a model three thou-sand miles over the water. Modern captains of industry might surprise Hamilton, modern cities shock him, and the power of industrial labor frighten him: for Hamilton never quite under-stood the transmitting power of social change, which in its opera-tion is more miraculous than scientific. Like Dr. Faustus' manser-vant, Hamilton could evoke elementals; but once materialized, that new industrialism swept away from the control of eighteenth-century virtuosos like the masterful Secretary of the Treasury. . . .
>
> Hamilton was a straggler behind his age, rather than the prophet of a new day. By a very curious coincidence, this old-fangled grand gentleman died from the bullet of Aaron Burr, friend and disciple of Bentham.

Thinkers whom Kirk sought to include, rather than exclude, from his canon sometimes met, however, more procrustean fates. It's fascinating to compare, for instance, the exegesis of a single sentence of Edmund Burke's both by Kirk and by Conor Cruise O'Brien in his recent study, *The Great Melody*. First, Kirk:

"I heaved the lead every inch of the way I made," Burke observed of his career, in the *Letter to a Noble Lord*. Heaving the lead is not a practice for which Irish orators are renowned; Burke's flights of eloquent fancy everyone knows; and surely Burke did not seem at Hasting's trial, to frightened Tory spectators, a man sworn to cautious plumbing of the depths. Yet Burke spoke accurately of his general policy as a statesman, for he based his every important decision upon a close examination of particulars. He detested "abstraction"—by which he meant not *principle*, but rather vainglorious generalization without respect for human frailty and the particular circumstances of an age and nation. Thus it was that while he believed in the rights of Englishmen and in certain human rights of universal application, he despised the "Rights of Man" which Paine and the French doctrinaires were soon to proclaim inviolable.

Now O'Brien.

The occasion for the composition of *Letter to a Noble Lord* was an attack by two Whig peers, the Duke of Bedford and the Earl of Lauderdale, in the Lords on 13 November 1795 on the pension which had been granted to Burke in the previous year, on his retirement from Parliament. . . . It enabled Edmund to pay his debts and to be assured, during his last illness, that his widow would not have to face a life of poverty. . . .

Inevitably, Burke's many enemies, among the Whigs and the radicals, triumphed. . . . It was the thirty pieces of silver. . . . Burke had received an enormous amount of abuse and innuendo—more than any other politician—in his long political career. In *Letter to a Noble Lord* he called it "the hunt of obloquy, which ever has pursued me with full cry through life." Most of those attacks came from anonymous writers in the corrupt press of the time, faceless and unaccountable tormenters. Burke did not answer those ever. The Duke of Bedford, on the other hand, was a marvelous target. . . .

He was also vulnerable. The Bedford family, since the days of Henry VIII, had been beneficiaries of Crown patronage on a colossal scale. Thus, by attacking Burke's modest pension, the Duke had unwittingly laid himself open to the most devastating *argumentum ad hominem* in the history of English controversy. . . . It contains [in the "heaving the lead" passage], with much else, Burke's grave and succinct rebuttal to the charge of venality that dogged him throughout his life, and has clung to his reputation ever since.

In some respects, obviously, Kirk's reading of the sentence is better. Kirk never even acknowledged, much less succumbed to, the contemporary urge to psychologize and personalize every human utterance. His Burke is a public man, and a public man's public statements are given public meanings by Kirk. Too, Kirk relies only on what he can see in the documentary record; O'Brien's conviction that he possesses some special intuition into Burke's Irish soul that justifies leaps beyond the available facts would have irritated Kirk no end. Even so, and for all that, O'Brien's Burke is a *man*—maybe a badly misunderstood man, but a man all the same. Kirk's Burke is a repository of political wisdom, the author of a series of preternatural insights on which, two hundred years later, a political movement can be grounded.

Russell Kirk has always reminded me of those nineteenth-century Central European historians who promoted national consciousness by writing passionate histories of "nations" that had not existed until those same historians invented them. And just as the nationalist historians manufactured "Croatia" or "Czechoslovakia" out of half-forgotten medieval and baroque fragments, Russell Kirk inspired the postwar conservative movement by pulling together a series of only partially related ideas and events into a coherent narrative—even, although Kirk objected to the word, into an ideology. Kirk did not record the past; he created it. He gathered the words of his political exemplars to answer his burning question:

> What is the essence of British and American conservatism? What system of ideas, common to England and the United States, has sustained men of conservative instincts in their resistance against radical theories and social transformation since the beginning of the French revolution?

As a question, of course, Kirk's query takes far too much for granted. Can one in fact fuse the English and American political traditions together in this way? Was the dilemma of the English Tories—how to maintain aristocratic deference in a democratizing society?—truly identical to that of American conservatives in the North—how to maintain the virtues of the founders' way of life in the face of colossal, unexpected wealth and exploding, non-Anglo-Saxon, populations?—and South—how to preserve white supremacy in the face of Northern criticism and an agricultural way of life in an industrial age? But Kirk's question is not a question. It is a prelude to a romantic reading of the past for the purposes of the present. No wonder, then, that *The Conservative Mind* found little favor with professional historians. Writers of the Left may be able to get away with devising "usable pasts": certainly Michel Foucault and the writers of women's history distort the past for their own polemical purposes on a scale and with a brazen falsity that would have made Kirk gasp. But in the hostile purlieus of the academy, writers of the Right must be more careful.

Yet if Kirk's great work cannot be counted as history, exactly, it ought to be esteemed as something in some ways more important: a profound critique of contemporary mass society, and a vivid and poetic image—not a program, an image—of how that society might better itself. It is, in important respects, the twentieth century's own version of the *Reflections on the Revolution in France*. If Kirk was not a historian, he was an artist, a visionary, almost a prophet. As long as he lived, by word and example he cautioned conservatives against over-indulging their fascination with economics. He taught that conservatism was above all a *moral* cause: one devoted to the preservation of the priceless heritage of Western civilization.

The Sensible
Philosopher

Of all the great teachers of mankind, can any have lived a duller life than Adam Smith? Between his birth in 1723 and his death in 1790, he seems to have done nothing but read, lecture, travel once to Europe as tutor to a young duke, hold a job as a customs commissioner, and (of course) write.

Nor did he leave behind a record of a particularly interesting personality. His books occasionally glint with wry wit, but Smith himself seems to have been a singularly unamusing man. As a young schoolteacher in Smith's home village of Kirkcaldy, Thomas Carlyle—not exactly a barrel of laughs himself—complained of a dinner given in honor of the birthday of the wife of Smith's aristocratic pupil, "The Fare was Sumptuous, but the Company was formal and Dull. Adam Smith their only Familiar at Table, was but ill qualifi'd to promote the Jollity of a Birthday . . . " Carlyle's assessment was echoed even by Smith's friends, who, though praising his kindliness, did warn new acquaintances about the economist's propensity for collaring people at parties and lecturing them unstoppably.

Smith, in other words, did not leave very much for a biographer to work with. If the new biography of Adam Smith by Professor Ian Ross—the first in a century—is tedious almost beyond endurance, the fault is not entirely the author's. Professor Ross has painstakingly gathered and sifted all the facts of Smith's life; he has dutifully performed a task for which other academics will be grateful. The book is not, however, one that will be read for or with pleasure.

It's a sadly missed opportunity. How Adam Smith came to think as he did is a question that probably never mattered more than it does now. Not since the original publication of *The Wealth of Nations* in 1776 have as many countries attempted the painful transition from statism to freedom as in our day. More than ever before, Adam Smith must be reckoned the most influential political thinker of the modern world. At the same time, he retains the distinction of being the most reviled one. From the halls of the French bureaucracy to the seminar rooms of midwestern universities, from the mosques of Qom to the mansions of Sir James Goldsmith, Smith stands accused of a litany of monstrous crimes: destroying revered ways of life and oppressing women, ignoring God's law and imposing an allegedly near-totalitarian monopoly of "neo-liberal" thought. Almost every grievance our world contains sooner or later turns into an indictment of this gentle Scotsman.

What has offended Smith's critics, past and present, is not Smith's supposed defense of selfishness and egotism; proponents of much more extreme and violent egotism—Friedrich Nietzsche, the pop psychologists of the 1960s and 1970s—elicit nowhere near as much dislike. Smith has been regarded as obnoxious, not because he advocates egotism, but because he takes it for granted as an inescapable fact of human character, and then suggests the means by which a virtuous society can put that fact to use. Smith, in a sense, falls between two camps. Those who dream of a harmonious social order, like feminists and Marxists, are affronted by his appraisal of human nature as unavoidably self-interested. On the other hand, those willing to accept a darker reading of human nature, like Michel Foucault and other students of Nietzsche, loathe Smith's prim vision of an invisible hand subduing the individual will and leading free individuals toward mutual cooperation. Smith is both anti-utopian and anti-Promethean; his work rebukes the loftiest of dreams and the most desperate of desires. It's a wonder, really, that there's anybody willing to buy a necktie with his profile on it.

Some eyebrows may rise at the suggestion that the author of *The Wealth of Nations* should be considered a political philosopher. Smith's masterwork devotes most of its energy to an attack on British commercial policies abandoned a century and a half ago. It's packed with frequently dry discussions of what seem to be technical issues. It scarcely bothers to address all sorts of questions that might be considered fundamental to its argument, including the most fundamental of all: why is wealth good? And as a result, like many of the philosophers who have written in English—such as Locke and Madison, Dicey and Hayek—Smith has usually been considered something less than *salonfähig* by the directors of admissions to the departments of political theory. Smith, like his Scottish and English colleagues, seems so commonplace and contented, so unwilling to grapple with the dark and morbid aspects of human personality, so hostile to the lofty and the adventuresome, so readily accessible to the casual reader and so uninterested in metaphysics. Nietzsche and Heidegger, Macchiavelli and Hegel—those are the thinkers worthy of attention and respect.

And this attitude is by no means confined to ideological opponents of liberal democracy. The disciples of Leo Strauss express, if anything, an even more patronizing attitude toward the authors of the political system that they as citizens wholeheartedly endorse. It's dangerously easy to forget that the real test of a political thinker is not the complexity and ingenuity of his reasoning, but the effect of his ideas when applied in practice. If you wouldn't care for a moment to live in the sort of world imagined by Plato or Heidegger, what on earth does it mean to say that you regard those two men as more substantial thinkers than sensible old Smith?

Judge by results. Smith deserves to be taken seriously, not just as a guide to public policy but as a thinker about politics. In order to take him seriously, though, we must first take seriously the questions that mattered to him. And it is here that we could have used a little more help from his biographer.

Smith was born in a poor country that had only recently been annexed by a vastly wealthier one. On both sides of the Anglo-Scottish border, most of the wealth belonged to people who either descended from successful practitioners of violence or courtiers who had been rewarded by enormous gifts from the Crown. It was a world that most of us now would regard as a horribly unjust one, and, in at least one way, it seemed to be getting worse. Over Smith's lifetime, Europe, and especially England, enjoyed a huge growth in trade and prosperity. Some of that new wealth did indeed trickle down to the people who needed it most, but pathetically little. Inspired by the example of their social betters, the growing class of merchants figured out that the fastest and safest route to wealth lay through government favoritism; in the name of national security, they demanded and received a barrage of monopolies, tariff exclusions, and special favors at the expense of the consumers of their products. We call this system of organized plunder "mercantilism," and it is not without its apologists even today.

Smith was a man of the Enlightenment, an intimate of David

Hume and a friend of Voltaire. (A new paper by Professor Samuel Fleischacker of Williams College demonstrates that he was also a major intellectual influence on Immanuel Kant.) He shared that too-often-maligned era's hatred of unnecessary suffering. At the same time, he understood its disdain for empty sentimentality, a disdain as alien to our own time as the era's powdered wigs.

Smith observed in the *Theory of Moral Sentiments* that

> if you would implant public virtue in the breast of him who seems heedless of his country, it will often be to no purpose to tell him, what superior advantages the inhabitants of a well-governed state enjoy; that they are better lodged, that they are better clothed, that they are better fed. These considerations will commonly make no great impression. You will be more likely to persuade, if you describe the great system of public police which procures these advantages, if you explain the connexions and dependencies of its several parts, their mutual subordination to one another, and their general subserviency to the happiness of society; if you show how this system might be introduced into his own country, what it is that hinders it from taking place there at present, how these obstructions might be removed, and all the several wheels of the machinery of government be made to move with more harmony and smoothness, without grating upon one another, or mutually retarding one another's motions. It is scarce possible that a man should listen to a discourse of this kind, and not feel himself animated to some degree of public spirit. He will, at least for the moment, feel some desire to remove those obstructions, and to put into motion so beautiful and so orderly a machine.

The Wealth of Nations likewise represents itself as concerned not with the suffering and happiness of the individual but with the strength of the state. "In modern war the great expence [sic] of fire-arms gives an evident to the nation which can best afford that expence . . . " Money, says Smith, wins wars. In a misguided attempt to obtain this war-winning money, nations have heaped restrictions on trade—incidentally impoverishing their poorest citizens. But the truth is that it's freedom of trade that produces national wealth and thus national security; and, incidentally, relieves want and raises wages.

Smith will concede, when confronted with a particularly stubborn mercantilist prejudice (such as England's Navigation Acts, which—like the still-surviving Jones Act in the U.S.—required goods carried between English ports to be carried on English ships), that "defense is more important than opulence." But the concession, even if sincere, is quickly withdrawn. Smith deftly discredits old-republican fantasies that it's anything other than "opulence" that determines the strength of a nation's defenses. Smith observed in one of his lectures on jurisprudence, cited by Ross, that "in the year 1745, four or five thousand naked Highlanders took possession of the improved parts of this country [Scotland] without any opposition from the unwarlike inhabitants. They penetrated into England and alarmed the whole nation, and had they not been opposed by a standing army they would have seized the throne with little difficulty." But of course, the Highlanders *were* opposed by a standing army, because rich nations can afford to raise them.

What rich nations can also afford to do—what they cannot help doing—is to distribute the benefits of wealth ever more widely. When we read accounts of the first impact of the Industrial Revolution in England, when we see the same process unleashed in Colombo or Shanghai, we are naturally appalled. Our horror, though, testifies principally to our ignorance of the even more hideous poverty that prevailed beforehand. The benefits that the English poor earned by moving from the countryside to the slums of the new cities are heartbreaking in their humility—earthenware instead of wooden plates, underwear, tea, and sugar—but they aren't any less real for their littleness. Neither are the scarcely less humble acquisitions of the toiling poor of East Asia and Central America. A bicycle, a radio, a package of aspirin, some pork with their rice, shoes rather than sandals: for these things, villagers worldwide are delighted to shatter what has been glamorized as "the world we have lost." Good riddance, they say with Smith. Who can find it in his heart to disagree with them?

Some critics of Smith's economics complain that the economic freedom he praised liberates a community-destroying acquisitiveness. Smith was no apologist for greed. His teaching at Glasgow University had brought him into contact with the merchants of that town, and he didn't care for them one bit. He much preferred the company of landowners. But Smith also knew that acquisitiveness was an indelible human characteristic. That's what he meant by his celebrated observation that "it is not from the benevolence of the butcher, the brewer, or the baker that we expect our dinner." He would not have been impressed for one moment by the argument, floated by some contemporary adherents of what's euphemistically called "communitarianism," that we eliminate greed by diverting the focus of acquisitiveness from productive enterprise to bureaucratic machinations.

Smith's great insight was that self-interest can be put to use by a virtuous society. Others had made similar points before—Mandeville in his *Fable of the Bees*, for example—but with a crucial difference of emphasis. Smith's predecessors argued that the profusion and waste of the rich brought a living to the poor. They might be described as proto-Keynesians. Smith's message was less cynical. If you reduce the number of opportunities to accumulate wealth through exploitation of the political system, you can confine acquisitiveness to the realm where it can do the most good: the elaboration of the principle of the division of labor.

Jerry Z. Muller, in his interesting book *Adam Smith in His Time and Ours*, contends that Smith presupposed certain social virtues as a prerequisite for an effective and just market economy. But one can equally well take the opposite point of view. A society committed to a market economy can also *promote*—without ever consciously meaning to—social virtues by proscribing in advance the unjust enrichment that pervades statist regimes: regimes like those that Smith observed throughout Europe. Smith chopped to pieces the classical cliché that wealth inevitably led to corruption and decadence. He showed that the same rules that led to economic growth could also inculcate civic virtue by inoculating the body politic against the corruption and injustice of monopoly—while also raising to decency and dignity the impoverished poor for whom classical political philosophy cared so little.

The Ross biography does not show us Smith's thought in progress; how his attention was directed to economic problems and the steps by which he developed the analysis that governs the world still. We do learn from it who the dons of Balliol College were when Smith was in attendance there, and I suppose somebody will want to know that. We learn a great deal about the building activities of Smith's father's friends, and I'm sure that information also answers some crying academic need.

But who and what Smith really was, why he thought as he did, and how he formed the generous and serene philosophy that makes the late twentieth century, for all its faults, such an agreeable place to live for hundreds of millions of human beings—the answers to those questions, it seems, must wait a while longer yet.

The Nietzsche of
Economics

During the writing of his biography of Mountbatten, Philip Ziegler posted a little reminder to himself above his desk: "Despite everything, he was a great man." Unfortunately for the anecdote, in Mountbatten's case the reminder was untrue. It would have made for a much better story had the note been written by Lord Robert Skidelsky to guide him as he chronicled the life of John Maynard Keynes.

Keynes was one of the most influential thinkers of our century, and his influence has been almost entirely bad. Since time immemorial, governments have debased their currency, misappropriated their people's wealth, and diverted the proceeds from productive investment to garish monuments to themselves. It was Keynes who supplied governments with arguments—and since Keynes was Keynes, brilliant arguments—to *justify* this outrageous conduct. If John Maynard Keynes had never lived, the Western world might still be the overtaxed, inflationary, statist mess that it is, but at least the people responsible for the mess would have to pretend to be embarrassed about it.

Instead, Keynes's fertile and subtle mind manufactured a huge armory of clever defenses of bad public policy. Since the publication of his 1936 masterwork, *The General Theory of Employment, Interest, and Money*, opponents of profligacy in government and state manipulation of the economy have had to contend not merely with the usual selfishness and cowardice of politicians' but also with the subversive power of Keynes's mordant and glittering mind.

Keynes did for economics what Nietzsche did for morals: he demonstrated that the absolute moral truths that earlier generations believed in were merely intellectual constructs, and constructs that could do with a great deal of improvement. Pre-Keynesian economics saw economies as naturally self-adjusting. Whatever dislocations and disturbances might flare up from time to time, over the long run an economy would perform as well as the skill, effort, and accumulated capital of the community permitted. This was the complacent theorem that provoked Keynes's famous jeer that "in the long run we are all dead."

Keynes argued that economies could underperform their potential for worryingly long periods of time, and that their tendency toward underperformance had grown worse since 1914. The problem was money: in the frightening post-Armistice world, wealth-owners too often held their wealth in cash, handy in case of emergency. According to pre-Keynesian orthodoxy, this was no problem: if the owners of wealth did not invest it, the banks in which they stored it would lend to someone who would. If large numbers of wealth-owners succumbed to the jitters, the amount of cash in banks would grow; with cash plentiful, interest rates would fall; and falling interest rates would encourage entrepreneurs to borrow and get the economy moving again. Keynes argued that this happy cycle need not occur—at any rate, it could not always be relied on to occur. A pound saved was, he contended, not automatically and by necessity a pound invested. It was potentially a pound stolen from productive purposes, a pound buried in the dark and denied to those who could put it to use.

Keynes prescribed two principal policies to set capital to work in a stagnant economy. First, interest rates must as a general rule be kept low, so as to minimize the temptation to hoard. (The "euthanasia of the rentier.") Second, governments must be prepared to invest directly in the economy to make up for the faint-heartedness of private businessmen. Keynes astutely foresaw that this combination of cheap money and lavish government expenditure could lead to trouble—inflation, depreciation of the currency, and so on. He was more than willing to sanction extraordinary interventions in economic life, including protective tariffs, in order to head those troubles off.

Some of the more conservative admirers of Keynes—dazzled by his vaulting imagination, his many valid insights, and his gorgeous literary style—have tried to salvage him for the cause of sound economics by insisting that his "general theory" was not really general at all. It was a *special* theory, adapted to the peculiar situation of Britain in the sluggish 1920s and grim 1930s. Just as Einstein conceded that Newtonian physics worked pretty well most of the time, only needing the help of the theory of relativity at very high speeds, so too, say conservative Keynesians, did Keynes accept the validity of classical market economics under normal conditions. But that's not how Keynes himself saw things, according to Skidelsky. Keynes was a temperamental radical, who relished the thought that he had overturned and rendered obsolete the entire existing structure of economics.

Skidelsky's first volume documented Keynes's animosity to the Victorian order of things, not just in economics but in all aspects of life. Keynes never escaped the self-congratulatory world of Bloomsbury—a sanctuary from which Edwardian aesthetes, emancipated women, and homosexuals poured condescending scorn on the philistinism and stupidity they perceived to surround them. Skidelsky plainly finds Bloomsbury a great deal less appealing than its zillions of contemporary chroniclers do. In both volumes of the biography he approvingly quotes Keynes's 1938 lecture "My Early Beliefs" as proof that the economist outgrew the callow ideas of the Cambridge Apostles and Gordon Square. "In retrospect," Skidelsky wrote in Volume I,

> Keynes felt that "his early beliefs" had brought him both gain and loss. The gain was that "we were amongst the first of our generation, perhaps alone amongst our generation[,] to escape from Benthamite tradition," with its "over-valuation of the economic criterion." This had protected "the whole lot of us from the final *reductio ad absurdum* of Benthamism known as Marxism." The loss lay in a "disastrously mistaken" view of human nature. He and his friends, repudiating original sin, had believed that human beings were sufficiently rational to be "released from . . . inflexible rules of conduct, and left, from now onwards, to their own . . . reliable intuitions of the good." This view ignored the fact that "civilisation was a thin and precarious crust erected by the personality and will of the few, and only maintained by rules and conventions skillfully put across and guilefully preserved."

Unfortunately, it's not clear that Keynes fully lived up to this more mature point of view. He went to his death caring more for the good opinion of Vanessa Bell and Lytton Strachey than that of anyone other than (just possibly) his wife. To the end he was a scoffer and a sneerer. Skidelsky does not deny this aspect of Keynes's personality, but he offers the ingenious defense that Keynes "was not, after all, improbably cast as 'the savior of capitalism.' Social systems are never saved by true believers, the virtues appropriate to going down with the ship rarely being suitable for the arts of navigation."

Of course, in one of history's too-obvious ironies, Keynesianism in due time evolved into a social system as calcified as Victorian capitalism, and Keynes's intellectual legacy came to be defended by true believers every bit as willing to go down with the ship as the hardfaced mid-nineteenth-century disciples of David Ricardo. Without being too fanciful, one can even say that Skidelsky's two volumes about Keynes eerily parallel Keynes's own writings. Keynes first important work, *The Economic Consequences of the Peace*, was published in 1920, while the world made by nineteenth-century capitalism lay shattered by the catastrophe of the First World War, but before men's minds had yet caught up. When Skidelsky's first volume was published in 1983, the world made by Keynesian demand-management and artificially cheap money was likewise a wreck, the victim of stagflation and the near-meltdown of the world banking system in August 1982. By the time Keynes's *General Theory* was put out, nineteenth-century economics was as defunct intellectually as it had been practically sixteen years before. And in the same way, as Skidelsky's second volume appears in the post–Berlin Wall era, Keynesianism has not only stopped working, it is nearly universally seen to have stopped working. The scoffer and sneerer is himself now scoffed at and sneered at.

Perhaps the most interesting thing about Skidelsky's biography—and it's packed with interesting things—is the author's willingness to grapple with this movement of economic thought away from Keynes. The entry for Hayek in the index of Volume II is twice as long as the entry for Marx. It is the right-wing criticisms of Keynes that Skidelsky anticipates and attempts to answer. He is at pains to show that Keynes did indeed appreciate the dangers of inflation, that he welcomed entrepreneurship, that he opposed excessive taxation, and that he attached virtually no value to equality as an end in itself. As Skidelsky tells it, Keynes may have disliked Britain's particular inequalities, which put a decadent landed class at the top, but he emphatically did not want to level individuals. In a particularly pungent mood, Keynes declared, "I do not want to antagonize the successful, the exceptional. I believe that man for man the middle class and even the upper class is very much superior to the working class." At times, Skidelsky's Keynes sounds oddly like a contemporary neoconservative: if the economy of postwar Europe stuttered and stammered, it was—Skidelsky's Keynes perceives—because the virtues that had made the nineteenth-century economy work had been blasted out of existence in 1914–18. Skidelsky's Keynes believes that the Victorian economy worked not because it complied with the laws of economics but because Victorian personalities made it work. Post-Victorian personalities, which Skidelsky's Keynes finds rather less admirable than some other Keyneses, had lost their forefathers' virtues and therefore required a new kind of economy—a more authoritarian economy, one that allowed weaker characters less scope. Skidelsky quotes from Virginia Woolf's diaries an account of a dinner in honor of T. S. Eliot in 1934. "I begin to see," Keynes said to Woolf, "that our generation—yours & mine . . . owed a great deal to our father's religion. And the young, like Julian [the son of Woolf's sister Vanessa Bell], who are brought up without it, will never get so much out of life. They're trivial: like dogs in their lusts."

For all its eloquence and impressive textual authority, for all its generous willingness to take seriously critics of Keynes whom Keynesians laughed at until little more than a decade ago, Skidelsky's attempted rescue of Keynes's economics founders on the single greatest practical deficiency of Keynesian policy: its blind faith in the wisdom, justice, and competence of civil servants. At some deep level, Keynes seems to have divided the world into two groups: people like himself and his Cambridge friends—intelligent, aesthetically sensitive, imbued with advanced opinions—and people like the despised "hearties" of his undergraduate days—athletic, stolid, conventional. In his mind, the first group was more naturally attracted to government, the second to business. And he had no doubt as to which group was more to be trusted. As scathing and funny as he could be about the investment decisions that businessmen might make with their own wealth, it never occurred to him to ponder with equal skepticism what clever art-loving grown-up undergraduates might do with other people's wealth.

At some level, this great man—a man who dedicated himself to ruthless truth-telling, no matter what the consequences; a man who put workability and the evidence of experience at the very center of his personal thought—can fairly be convicted of the error that would have appalled him most: naïveté. Damningly, his naïveté was born not out of ignorance or gullibility but out of vanity. He was naïve about government, and the risk of governmental error, because he expected that the upper reaches of government would be staffed by men rather like himself, in sensibility if not in genius. Skidelsky calls Keynes the last of the great English liberals. In at least one sense, the accolade—if it is an accolade—is well deserved. Despite the condemnation of precisely this sort of error in "My Early Beliefs," Keynes could never shake himself free of the prejudice that the world was governed by more or less reasonable chaps, and that no part of the world was more likely to be governed by reasonable chaps than one's nation's enemies.

As a senior Treasury official in the First World War, Keynes was an important organizer of British survival and the eventual Allied victory. But all through the war he held fast to the pacifist dogma that the military rulers of Germany wanted a compromise peace every bit as much as Bloomsbury did. "Indeed," Skidelsky comments sadly, "a gross overestimate of the strength of the German moderates, as well as a misunderstanding of their aims, was characteristic of the whole British middle-class peace movement." They projected their own image upon a hostile and dangerous world. If not naïveté, this was at least narcissism—an involvement with oneself so all-consuming that one could not absorb the information that other people held radically different opinions and behaved in entirely different ways. It is this weakness, more than any other trait of Keynes's, that convinces this reader of his biography that, had Keynes somehow survived to a riper age, he would never have migrated rightward, no matter what his more conservative admirers claim. A liberal Keynes was, a liberal he would have remained.

But give Keynes credit for this: Keynes showed no such naïveté in the 1930s. He grasped the Nazi menace from the start, and shot the Labour Party's arguments to pieces when it espoused fear of budget deficits as a reason to oppose British re-armament. Nor, aside from a brief flurry of over-optimism about the prospects for relatively rapid economic growth in Russia as a result of a visit there in 1925, was Keynes ever seduced by communism. "Marxist socialism," he wrote in 1924, "must always remain a portent to the historians of opinion—how a doctrine so illogical and so dull can have exercised so powerful and enduring influence over the minds of men and, through them, the course of history." A decade later, he was warning Cambridge undergraduates that Marxism stood far below Social Credit as economic quackery, and mischievously wrote to George Bernard Shaw:

> My feelings about *Das Kapital* are the same as my feelings about the Koran. I know that it is historically important and I know that many people, not all of whom are idiots, find it a sort of Rock of Ages and containing inspiration. Yet when I look into it, it is to me inexplicable that it can have this effect. Its dreary, out-of-date, academic controversialising seems so extraordinarily unsuitable as material for the purpose . . . How could either of these books carry fire and sword round half the world? It beats me.

Despite his mockery, Keynes well understood the attractions of communism to the affluent young. "When Cambridge undergraduates take their inevitable trip to Bolshiedom, are they disillusioned when they find it all dreadfully uncomfortable? Of course not. That is what they are looking for." In his liberal way, however, he found the conversion to Marxism comical rather than horrifying.

As Keynes's funny but deadly animadversions on Marxism suggest, much of the impact of his ideas originated in his remarkable personal charm. In a small society like that of interwar England, personality counted. And Keynes's was evidently delightful. He treated his Bloomsbury friends with extraordinary generosity, generosity that was seldom returned. Cambridge followed his ideas at least in part because it liked him so much. It makes one wonder whether the course of modern economic life would have been different had Ludwig von Mises not been such a pedantic and irascible old man, or if Hayek had been quicker with a joke.

To Skidelsky's credit, much of Keynes's charm is captured on the page, which one would think would be an almost impossible task. But then, Skidelsky accomplishes one impossible task right after another. His biography combines the telling of Keynes's fascinating life with penetrating and surprisingly accessible analysis of Keynes's economic ideas, of his times, of the philosophy from which his work proceeded. (More technical discussions are appended to the ends of the appropriate chapters.) Along the way, Skidelsky pauses for some illuminating reflection on the biographer's historiography.

> An inescapable conundrum of biography is to know what allowance to make for the *Zeitgeist* in directing one's subject's thought and life. People are children of their times, as well as of

> their parents. . . . But the implicit biographical assumption is that
> for most explanatory purposes, the *Zeitgeist* can be held constant;
> that it changes more slowly than the individual life; and that,
> therefore, family, education and class are the main systematic
> external influences the biographer needs to consider. . . . The
> assumption . . . is that biographical subjects are much more fre-
> quently products of their *backgrounds* than of their *times*.

In Keynes's case at least, Skidelsky maintains, the usual assumption
is wrong.

Altogether, this is a very successful biography. Is it too long?
Biographies nowadays nearly always are. I sometimes wonder
whether excessively long biographies are not a side effect of the
decline of public sculpture. The Victorians gave their heroes stat-
ues; we don't know how to do that anymore, and so we build our
monuments in bookshop windows. But long as it is, this is a book
worth the time it consumes. The reader who works his way
through it will emerge with a keener understanding not just of Keynes's time, but of his own.

The Uses of Resentment

What is one to make of Kevin Phillips? The man who is widely regarded as the greatest living expert on American electoral politics is a mixture of political insight and economic preposterousness; deep historical knowledge and glib sound bites; respect for American traditions and hostility to American institutions. At moments, he writes with the authority of the expert; pages later, he is touting nonsense with the unscrupulousness of an infomercial charlatan.

Phillips's latest book, *Arrogant Capital*, unfortunately exhibits rather more of his flaws than his abilities. *Arrogant Capital* is the third in a series of books about what Phillips calls "the Reagan aftermath"—following *The Politics of Rich and Poor* (1990) and *Boiling Point* (1993)—and it is considerably the slightest of the three. Phillips has often made misleading use of simplistic historical analogies, and he indulges himself with special verve here. Not content with analogizing America's alleging decline to that of Edwardian Britain, eighteenth-century Holland, and Hapsburg Spain in *Boiling Point*, he has now added the even more noncomparable case of Imperial Rome for good measure. He seriously offers up the following pop-numerology to the credulous reader:

> Internationally, end-of-the century decades have often been eventful ones—the 1490s, the 1690s, and 1790s come to mind. . . . Spaniards started getting worried about the future in the 1590s, and Dutch concern accelerated in the 1690s. British uncertainty, in turn, mushroomed in the 1890s. . . . [F]or citizens of this country, the nineties have a second, more encouraging tradition—one already fulfilled twice. The nineties have been prime periods of American political and ideological revolution, as opposed to physical and military upheaval. The 1790s, which began with the essentially conservative triumph of the Constitu-

185

tion and its ratification, finished with something very different: the renewal of anti-elite politics, the election of Thomas Jefferson, and the "Revolution of 1800." A century later, the 1890s, which began with robber-baron capitalism and laissez-faire at its zenith, ended with populism and progressivism on the rise.

Hmmm. What about this parallel observation: The forties of every one of the past five centuries have suffered major international convulsions: World War II in the twentieth century, the revolutions of 1848 in the nineteenth, the War of the Austrian Succession in the eighteenth, the bitterest phase of the Thirty Years War in the seventeenth, religious strife throughout the Holy Roman Empire in the sixteenth. Coincidence? Well, actually, yes.

These outbreaks of silliness from so keenly intelligent a man as Phillips suggest that *Arrogant Capital* was written in considerable haste, in a frantic attempt to call back the big bet Phillips placed on Bill Clinton in the 1993 book:

> The 1992 results could be interpreted as a Democratic watershed. . . . [A] new set of domestic and cultural issues were emerging for the 1990s: health care, education, urban problems, the environment, economic fairness, abortion and what could be called a 'women's' array of concerns, including day care, parental leave, equal pay, the feminization of poverty, the glass ceiling in employment, women's political empowerment and sexual harassment. Issues like these favored the Democrats, affirming that electoral watersheds usually overlap with new domestic-policy agendas.

Arrogant Capital begins by attempting to explain away that embarrassing misreading of the 1992 results. In the later book, Phillips insists that while he did predict "that the post-1968 GOP era would soon end in a populist reaction against both the increasingly unresponsive Washington elite and the economic redistribution of the 1980s in favor of the nation's rich," he did not "try to spell out [the reaction's] form or depth of success." Sadly, this eager attempt to catch the voters' mood on the rebound has proved no more successful than Phillips's last exercise in soothsaying: having wrongly hailed the ascendancy of the Democrats in his 1993 book, Phillips reversed himself and announced the imminent demise of *both* parties in the 1994 book—just months before the Republican congressional landslide.

Forecasting errors—an occupational hazard cheerfully accepted by most political journalists—are a serious matter for Phillips. More than most political writers, Phillips has advertised himself as a seer. The blurbs selected for the back cover of *Arrogant Capital*— a book written to smudge the wrong guesses of *Boiling Point*—all pay tribute to the uncanny accuracy of Phillips's past prognostications. In fact, his reputation for wizardry rests on his 1969 book *The Emerging Republican Majority.* Since then, the prophetic gift has largely deserted him.

On the other hand, what remains is in many ways more interesting. Phillips does not need to be a prophet to command attention. He is the unsurpassed master of the historical details of American electoral politics. Who but Kevin Phillips could casually drop the factoid that no county within forty miles of Washington, D.C., produced any significant vote for Abraham Lincoln in 1860? And Phillips has mastered something even more important still: he has made himself the explicator of—and apologist for—the darkest and most brooding emotions of the American voter.

Unlike his onetime idol Bill Clinton—who flatters himself that he represents the "politics of hope" against antagonists who represent "the politics of fear"—Phillips does not affect to regard the middle-class voter as a person of generous instincts. Phillips has always based his analysis on the premise that Americans vote their resentments. Back in the 1960s, he believed that they resented blacks, students, bureaucrats, and liberal judges; today he claims they resent Wall Street speculators, corporate chieftains, and Washington lobbyists. Always, though, he has maintained that the voters are seething with rage and envy, and that big political rewards can be grasped by politicians who can take advantage of those emotions. The political uses of resentment—that's what Phillips taught Richard Nixon in the 1960s, and it's what he has been attempting to teach Democrats and independent political entrepreneurs like Ross Perot in the 1990s.

"Hardly anyone doubts how angry the public is at 1990s Washington and what the city has become," he observes on *Arrogant Capital*'s very first page. Citing a survey by Democratic pollster Celinda Lake, Phillips notes that at the end of President Clinton's first year in office, 57 percent of Americans believed that "lobbyists and special interests" controlled Washington—up from 38 percent just two and a half years before.

One plausible explanation for this startling uptick in American cynicism—that the Clinton administration actually *was* under the control of lobbyists and special interests in a way that the two previous Republican administrations were not—would be scorned by Phillips. Phillips long ago ceased to regard the education lobby, big-city mayors, trade unions, feminists, civil rights organizations, and retirees as "special interests." Instead, Phillips thinks, the public is angry because the president they elected in a spasm of populist outrage has failed them. Despite Bill Clinton, Phillips maintains, a powerful and entrenched financial elite continues to exploit America's antiquated constitutional machinery to enrich itself and the foreign economic competitors with which it is allied, while impoverishing the middle class. What an unhappy contrast between the present day and the good old days of the early 1970s, "before the global economy was hooked up to supercomputers and changed to the megabyte standard," when "the financial sector was subordinate to Congress and the White House."

Here, as always when he comments on economic matters, Phillips's penetrating mind is gummed by nineteenth-century ideological dust. Like some long-buried Passionara of the Free Unlimited Coinage of Silver, Phillips contrasts the evils of international *Finanzkapital* with the craggy virtues of agriculture and manufacturing. The simplest and least conspiratorial explanation of the growing power of financial markets—which is that the out-of-control welfare states of the 1990s are borrowing far more money than the relatively well-managed economies of the 1960s—does not even rate a mention from him.

But then, Phillips isn't very much interested in explaining things. He inveighs against the litigation explosion and the burgeoning number of lawyers. But when he has to articulate a reason for this deplorable phenomenon, he stammers. "[T]here are simply too many attorneys, which forces them to keep generating legislative, regulatory, and litigational subject matter and opportunity." Too many lawyers, in other words, produce too many laws. Serious-minded critics of the legal profession—like, curiously enough, the dean of the Harvard Law School, Robert Clark—have demonstrated that the causality runs exactly the other way. A society that insists on emitting enormous numbers of laws and regulations will quickly enough find itself employing enormous numbers of experts to help citizens cope with those laws and regulations. The litigation explosion of the 1980s was merely an aftershock of the regulatory explosion of the 1970s.

The same indifference to serious explanations is manifested in

Phillips's account of the multiplication of bureaucrats and quasi-bureaucrats in Washington. He rattles off the numbers with appropriate alarm: 11,000 congressional staffers in 1970 vs. 20,000 in 1990; 19 percent of professional associations located in Washington in 1971 vs. 32 percent in 1990; 21,000 members of the District of Columbia bar in 1975 vs. 61,000 in 1993; 1,500 journalists working in the capital in 1950 vs. 12,000 today. But unlike other writers who have pondered these numbers—notably Jonathan Rauch in *Demosclerosis: The Silent Killer of American Government*—Phillips does not ask himself *what* all these people are doing and *why* non-Washingtonians are paying them to do it. He seems to regard his cancerous multiplication as an almost completely autochthonous phenomenon: "a bipartisan awareness, involving perhaps a hundred thousand people, that the city on the Potomac had become a golden honey pot for the politically involved." But of course, Washington has become such a honey pot precisely because its presidents and legislators have for thirty years followed the course that Phillips broadly favors—writing ever more complicated tax laws, regulating markets ever more closely, penalizing foreign exporters ever more heavily. When the political authorities in effect tell businesses, "get a lobbyist or we might destroy your company," it's hardly surprising that tens of thousands of businesses, across America and around the world, suddenly start employing people to take congressional staffers to lunch. The growth of Washington's professional population is a direct consequence of the growth of the federal government's appetite for power. Nobody who, like Phillips, favors further arrogations of power by that government has standing to complain about the size of the bureaucracy needed to exercise it—nor about the number of supplicants who flock to Washington to beg that this power be exercised in ways that help them and hobble their competitors.

Nowhere is the disjunction between cause and effect sharper—or more useful to Phillips—than in the long discussion of stagnant middle-class incomes that runs through all three of the books he has published in the past five years. Thus, in *The Politics of Rich and Poor* he amassed data showing (accurately) that the number of rich and very rich people increased sharply in the 1980s. In *Boiling Point*, he amassed more data purporting to show that the standard of living of middle-class Americans had stagnated. But Phillips conjured up scant evidence that these two sets of facts had anything to do with each other.

That might seem strange: After all, in the past—in the boom years from 1896 to 1917, for example, or in the 1920s—increases in the number and wealth of the best-off Americans have coincided with rising living standards for the middle class. Periods in which the number and wealth of the rich shrinks—such as the 1930s— have coincided with stagnating or falling middle-class living standards. In good times, all prosper, if unequally; in bad times, all suffer, if again unequally.

For many Americans, this old rule of thumb continued to work in the 1980s. Phillips complained in *Boiling Point* that the number of Americans in the "middle class" shrank by between five and ten percentage points in the 1980s. But far more American families were moving *upward* out of the middle class than downward. Of America's 66 million families, 17 million enjoyed incomes of $50,000 or more (1991 dollars) in 1980, and 22.3 million enjoyed such incomes in 1990. (The new prosperity coursed with special vitality through black America: only 810,000 black families brought in more than $50,000 in 1980; 1.3 million had crossed the threshold of comfort in 1990.)

On the other hand, it's also true that many Americans were moving downward, and that the income of the average household—a category that includes individuals living alone—has been stagnating at about $30,000 (1990 dollars) since 1969.

What's going on? A hundred and one things, but perhaps the most important of them is this: the collapse of the American family as a social unit. In 1980, 61 percent of American households were made up of married families. In 1992, only 55 percent were—an amazing shift. By grim contrast, the number of households in which a once-married woman lived without a husband jumped by 34 percent in the years from 1980 to 1992.

The economic implications of these changes in ways of life are huge. In 1991, 38 percent of all married-couple families enjoyed incomes over $50,000. Fewer than 8 percent of husbandless women earned so much. If you flip that number over, its implications are even more startling: of those households earning incomes of $50,000 or more, 81 percent were married families.

Family incomes grew rapidly between 1945 and 1973 largely because families themselves were so stable. Divorce rates were low, illegitimacy was rare, and most families sent only one wage-earner into the workforce. (A recent survey of corporate executives found evidence that men who are the sole support of their families work harder and longer than men whose wives also work. Perhaps it's the weight of responsibility, or perhaps when the wife is at home the husband can concentrate his energies more fully on the job.) Under those conditions, every extra dollar paid to a full-time worker translated into a higher income for his wife and children.

In an era of extreme family instability, however, economic growth does not suffice to enrich families. Dividing one income between two postdivorce households has, among other consequences, a depressing effect on national income statistics. And that's assuming the father can be induced to pay child support. If he refuses, the wife and children of a divorced father form a new, probably very low wage, household that depresses the national statistics even more deeply—as do the households of the millions of women whose boyfriends fathered children on them and then abandoned them to a weary life of welfare or minimum-wage labor.

None of this excites Phillips much. His attention is concentrated on the powerful political potential of the fact that many have suffered economically at a time when a few have prospered enormously. That disparity, in the hands of a clever pol, is a resentment that might be profitably galvanized, and wherever you detect resentment, you find Kevin Phillips there ahead of you.

Recognizing the truth that it's Big Government that spawns lobbyists and that it's social breakdown which is producing the dreary economic numbers against which Phillips rages makes nonsense of the ten-point reform package with which he ends *Arrogant Capital*. He recommends, for example, moving federal agencies out of Washington. "The Interior Department could be moved to Denver or Salt Lake City, Agriculture to Des Moines or Kansas City, Housing and Urban Development to Philadelphia or Chicago. Uprooted lobbies would mean broken lines of influence." To the contrary—moving agencies to smaller centers where they would quickly rank among the largest local employers and where they could go about their business far from the scrutiny of Congress and the national press would guarantee capture by special interest groups and doom forever any hope of shrinking the agencies' payrolls.

In the same heedless spirit, Phillips repeats University of Texas professor Steve Magee's suggestion that the number of people admitted to law schools each year should be shrunk in order to cap the lawyer explosion. But of course capping the number of lawyers without simultaneously choking the flow of laws and regulations would simply foster artificial scarcities and inflate the incomes of those lawyers now in practice.

As for Phillips's recommendation that the country attempt to raise the incomes of the middle class through protectionism and punitive new tax increases on corporations and high-income earners—all one can say is that it's been tried before, and with dismal results.

To engage with these ideas, however, is to fundamentally misunderstand them. Kevin Phillips is no more interested in the question of whether higher taxes will spark the economy than the designers of the '57 Chevy were interested in whether tail fins would in fact stabilize their car at high speeds. What Phillips cares about is devising formulas that can be put to use effectively by canny political operators. Despite the 1994 congressional results, his distinctive blend of nationalism and class resentment may yet prove to be just such a formula. And those of us who admire Phillips's immense talents—while deploring the dark uses to which he has devoted them—had better remain prepared to explain to an electorate enraged and frightened by the economic costs of social breakdown exactly why he's wrong.

The Palaces of Newport

I've been holidaying in the neighborhood where Edith Wharton set much of *The Age of Innocence*—Newport, Rhode Island, the gaudiest resort of the nineteenth century. And as one tours the marble mansions of the town, overlaid with one wild architectural extravagance after another, one question repeatedly recurs: what in the world did they think they were doing? Why did the industrialists of the nineteenth century feel compelled to build seventeenth-century palaces beside the Atlantic Ocean?

The usual answer, derived from Thorstein Veblen, a contemptuous contemporary observer, is that the very rich have always lavished their wealth on conspicuous consumption—a phrase Veblen invented. Just as the super-rich of the 1980s would buy Ferrari Testarossas and jet to Aspen in private planes, so the plutocracy of the 1880s built mansions in Newport in which to spend seven weeks of the year.

To my mind, Veblen's answer is not very helpful. Let's agree that rich people through the ages have spent money to over-awe the non-rich. Why did the over-awing ever take the apparently bizarre form of marble one hundred-bedroom "cottages?" Why, in 1994, does nobody, no matter how rich, build analogous structures?

Part of the explanation is that the millionaires of the 1880s were, relative to everyone else, much richer than the billionaires of today. The man who constructed the vastest of the Newport mansions, Cornelius Kissam Vanderbilt (grandson of the Cornelius Vanderbilt who created the New York Central Railway), inherited a fortune of some $100 million on his father's death in 1885. The value of the dollar in those days was fixed at one-twentieth of an ounce of gold; today it floats at roughly ⅕₅₀th. Theoretically, then, the builder of the Breakers inherited some $1.75 billion in modern money—a vast sum indeed, but no vaster than that possessed by the richest people of our day.

But now look at Vanderbilt's relative wealth. A skilled industrial worker in 1885 (like the engineers who drove Vanderbilt's locomotives) could hope to earn $1,000 a year, enough to house and support a family in dignity according to the standards of the day. Thus, Vanderbilt's fortune amounted to 100,000 times the annual wage of his best-paid blue-collar employee. Today a locomotive driver might gross $40,000. To equal Vanderbilt's purchasing power, the owner of a 1994 railroad would therefore require $40 billion. No individual in the world possesses wealth on anything remotely resembling that scale.

Once you grasp the incredible magnitude of the fortunes amassed in the United States between 1865 and 1914, the Newport cottages become more comprehensible. Until the 1860s, American society had diverged radically from that of Europe. Certainly, there were rich men, as well as clergymen, landed families, and professors who expected special respect. But America knew nothing like the aristocracy that lorded over nearly every European country.

Then, suddenly, there appeared a class of men who towered as high above their neighbors as any European prince or duke. To us now, this plutocracy looks like a bizarre historical anomaly; in 1885, it must have seemed that America was simply catching up with the rest of the civilized world.

The Vanderbilts and other great families of the day must have felt that they were treading the path trod by Florence's Medici or Britain's East India nabobs: from commercial wealth to aristocratic predominance. Which meant that the American plutocrats felt obliged to mimic the manners and rules of a European aristocracy. And on their European tours they had learned that the very first thing an aristocratic family needed was a grand ancestral mansion in the neoclassical style.

Of course, the American rich of the Gilded Age got the historical trend completely wrong. America and the world were evolving toward even greater social *equality*. The industrialization from which the Vanderbilts and their ilk gained their wealth was simultaneously corroding their position by dramatically raising the value and cost of labor. Houses built to last the centuries were either torn down or donated to the public by the children and grandchildren of the builders.

Blinded by the turmoil of events, man believes he perceives the future: in 1885 that future seemed to belong to capitalist aristocracy; today it seems to be computer-powered welfare capitalism. But it is almost certain that we are wrong, and that abstract forces all unnoticed are preparing a future for us entirely different from the one we are expecting.

Peter Taylor

The celebration of the 1994 Republican blowout is tinctured by sad news: the death the week before of a man who had ranked among the greatest—I would say, was the greatest—of living American writers, Peter Taylor. Taylor died November 2, 1994, in Charlottesville, Virginia, at the age of seventy-seven.

You may never have heard of Taylor. Up to a point, that was his own fault. Despite his span of life, he produced relatively little work: seven collections of short stories, three novels, some plays. His writings are, almost without exception, brilliant, but they are also undeniably scanty.

Still, it's not as if Bret Easton Ellis or Alice Walker—to cite only two of the more-hyped contemporary writers—have as yet published so very much more than Taylor did. If Ellis and Walker are celebrities while Taylor is not, it is largely because of the unfashionableness of his subject matter: the inner lives and memories of white southerners of what Taylor habitually refers to as "good family." The narrator of his final novel, for example, is the grandson of a U.S. senator, who was himself the great-grandson of a Revolutionary War general. More offensive still to modern sensibilities, is the way he writes about these characters: ironically, yes, critically, often, but always respectfully.

Of course, nobody but a bureaucrat or an academic could imagine that one has said anything much at all about a writer when one sums up the race and social class of his protagonists. What made Taylor a great writer was the remarkable sensibility he brought to bear on those protagonists: intensely local, soaked in the past, and always infused with awareness of the mystery that lurks around the corner.

The first sentence of his final novel gives you the idea: "In the Tennessee country of my forebears it was not uncommon for a man of good character suddenly to disappear." The rest of the book, naturally, is about just such a man. The narrator's increasingly obsessive efforts to find him in the end reveal to us more than merely a plot twist: they illuminate the life of the vanished Tennessee country of those ancient forebears.

For the central mystery in all Taylor's writing is time. A typical Taylor story is narrated by an old man, thinking back on events of his youth that in their turn cast light upon the even more remote past, as in this paragraph from my favorite of his stories, "In the Miro District":

> He was my maternal grandfather and was known to everyone as Major Basil Manley. Seeing Major Manley like that at the wheel of his tan touring car, swinging into our driveway, it wasn't hard to imagine how he had once looked riding horseback or muleback through the wilds of West Tennessee when he was a young boy in Forrest's cavalry, or how he had looked, for that matter, in 1912, nearly half a century after he had ridden with General Forrest, at the time when he escaped from a band of hooded nightriders who had kidnapped him then—him and his law partner (and who had murdered his law partner before his eyes, on the banks of the Bayou du Chien, near Reelfoot Lake). Even when I was a very small boy, I dreaded the sight of him . . .

And in a forty-five-page account of the struggle between this fierce old man and his unloving grandson, Taylor manages to tell more of the story of the Old South and the New than even the minutest of the region's historians.

Taylor did not go unrecognized in his lifetime. He won the Pulitzer Prize in 1987 and held prestigious teaching appointments at Harvard and the University of Virginia. His books were published under the respectable imprint of Alfred A. Knopf, in elegant editions. But in literature, the big prizes are awarded posthumously. And I believe that long after *The Color Purple* has been consigned to sit alongside *Little Men* on the shelf of unstomachably pious *écriture*, Peter Taylor will be remembered as the outstanding master of late-twentieth-century American fiction.

A Passover Seder

The feast of Passover is the most ancient of this planet's religious festivals. It was already ten centuries old when Jesus shared out his *matzah* and wine at the Passover seder the Christian world knows as the Last Supper. The liturgy read at Passover, the Haggadah, was completed twelve hundred years before Archbishop Cranmer composed the Book of Common Prayer, three hundred years before Mohammed unveiled the Koran.

The story told at Passover is that of the Exodus from Egypt, but in those immense periods of time, many other layers of meaning have accreted upon the holiday. Passover has been interpreted as a promise of life after death, with Egypt representing the rigors of life in this world and the land of Canaan as the paradisical world to come. It has been understood as a Jewish festival of national liberation, like the Fourth of July or Bastille Day. Some have construed it as a generalized celebration of freedom, in which the Jews stand in for all the world's oppressed and the Egyptians for all the world's oppressors.

What I find myself brooding about at Passover, however, is the aspect about the holiday that is perhaps the most troubling to the modern, secularized mind: the intervention of the divine into human history.

The Passover story is full of miracles—the burning bush, the ten plagues, the splitting of the Red Sea, the manna in the desert. Modern people simply don't believe in miracles: As the great skeptical philosopher David Hume acidly noted, it's far likelier the person who observed the alleged miracle erred (or lied) than that the laws of nature were violated. Even people who regard themselves as religious tend to adhere to some version of what the eighteenth century called the "watchmaker" theory: God made the universe, wound it up, and then set it ticking without it requiring any further involvement on His part.

At Passover, though, Jews repeat phrases which, if taken seriously, commit us to quite a different belief: to a belief that God can—and has—dramatically intervened in human affairs to shape history. It's possible, I suppose, to read those phrases without meaning them, as an antique preliminary to tucking into supper. But suppose one were to take them seriously for a moment?

The twentieth century has certainly not lacked for decisive events that changed history in ways that nobody could have predicted: the shooting of the Archduke Ferdinand in the streets of Sarajevo, the seizure of power in Petrograd by Lenin and the Bolsheviks, the failure of Britain and France to chase Germany out of the Rhineland in 1936, to name just three. The problem, for anyone who wants to see Providence at work, is that most of these startling occurrences have altered history for the worse. Had history continued to bubble along as expected in, say, the spring of 1914, how much happier would the lives of tens of millions have been!

But then, maybe the real problem is that we assume too quickly that the sign of the providential is a change for the better. The Exodus story echoes with complaints that remind us the Israelites did not always share Moses's conviction that he was improving their lives. "Were there no graves in Egypt that thou hast taken us away to die in the wilderness?" And, in the end, the generation that fled Egypt did all die in the wilderness, after forty years of wandering through the desert of Sinai.

In the thirty-seventh year of that bleak itinerary, the Israelites must have found it as difficult to muster confidence that history was unfolding in accordance with some divine plan as we do. And their experience suggests two important truths to modern people who despair of seeing any order or purpose in the flow of life: First, that what seems to an individual like an unbearably long delay—forty years of dust and heat—is but a very short time in the life of the human race. And second, that if there is such a thing as providential purposes, we should not hastily assume they include the comfort and prosperity of each and every generation.

We interpret suffering as proof there is no Providence, because we take for granted that God's purposes—if He has purposes—preclude suffering. Tell that to the Egyptians who lost their first-borns in the tenth plague. The Passover story reminds us of a very different truth: that God's purposes, if such exist, need not be the same as man's—and that perhaps we can see His presence in even the worst of human misery.

Index

201